How To Manifest Miracles In Your Life

bj King

How To Manifest Miracles In Your Life

bj King

Copyright © 2025 by bj King

Published by 1st World Publishing
P.O. Box 2211, Fairfield, Iowa 52556
tel: 641-209-5000 • fax: 866-440-5234
web: www.1stworldpublishing.com

First Edition

ISBN Softcover: 978-1-4218-3595-2

LCCN: Library of Congress Cataloging-in-Publication Data

All rights reserved. No part of this book may be reproduced or utilized in any form or by any means, electronic or mechanical, including photocopying or recording, or by any information storage and retrieval system, without permission in writing from the author.

This material has been written and published for educational purposes to enhance one's well-being. In regard to health issues, the information is not intended as a substitute for appropriate care and advice from health professionals, nor does it equate to the assumption of medical or any other form of liability on the part of the publisher or author. The publisher and author shall have neither liability nor responsibility to any person or entity with respect to loss, damages, or injury claimed to be caused directly or indirectly by any information in this book.

What I offer to you in this book are my own opinions and beliefs based on direct experiences with Spirit over the past forty years and information I've consolidated from reading Ancient Wisdom teachings. <u>These statements are not presented as THE TRUTH</u>. Do not accept what I have written as truth only as one person's opinion. <u>Accept only what resonates with your own discernment, your own truth</u>. Discernment is one of the spiritual gifts promised to us all. If you do not feel you have it, pray for it. All spiritual gifts are given to us as a result of our asking for them. <u>How you utilize the information in this book you do at your own risk, I accept no responsibility</u>.

Table of Contents

    Partnership agreement 6
1. Who are you and what on Earth are you Doing Here? 7
2. Find the Positive by Looking at the Negative 24
3. How to Gain Deliberate Control of Your Life 28
4. How to Manifest Miracles in Your Life 41
5. How to Create Your Version of Heaven on Earth 53
6. Our Emotions and Beliefs Affect Manifestation 79
7. Living Our Best Life 93
8. Attracting the Life We Desire 126

PARTNERSHIP AGREEMENT

I, _____(your name)_____, on this date, _____ do enter into an agreement of cooperation with the Holy Mother/Father God of Light.

I agree to recognize The Creator as my Source in all my relationships, both business and personal.

I agree to live from the definition, I AM God expressing itself through the personality of _____(your name)_____, for the benefit of Earth, all life on the Earth and beyond.

I agree to live my life intuitively, asking The Creator at all times, "What is the next single thing for me to do or know to be in a state of Divine Grace?"

I agree to gift a percentage of my monthly income to the physical source who assists me with my personal spiritual growth.

It is my desire to serve the Universe in the following manner:
1.
2.
3.
4.
5.
6.

I choose to be true to myself. I choose perfect health physically, mentally, emotionally and spiritually. I choose freedom. I choose to do God's will for my life.

I choose to serve the Universe with my gifts and talents. In exchange, I accept from the Universe, through the grace of God and to the highest good of all concerned, the fulfillment of my needs and desires.

This contract supersedes all previous agreements I have made with my Higher Self and is duly in force and operating for me now.

Signed:_____ Dated:_____

1.

Who Are You And What On Earth Are You Doing Here?

**We are here to expand spiritual energy in this dimension.
That is why we have come.
That is our purpose.**

We are all here because as souls, we chose to come to Earth. Our hearts beat with the energy of God. We are aspects of God in Human form. In the Bible it says we were made in the image and likeness of God, which means we are creators and capable of creating as God does. We were made by God, for God to use and until we understand that, life doesn't make as much sense. God is the Source of our lives. I have found it useful to think of myself in terms of: I AM God, operating through my personality for the benefit of Earth, all species of life on the Earth and beyond. You might want to write out this affirmation and include your name.

It is not fate, nor chance, nor luck, nor coincidence that we are living at this time. Our births were not mishaps or mistakes or a fluke of nature. Our parents may not have planned us, but God did.

<u>God says there are illegitimate parents, but there are no illegitimate children.</u>

As a teenager, I remember listening to Patty Page's song, "Ke Sera Sera, Whatever Will Be, Will Be," and wondering if that was true. Was my destiny already established and I had no control over my future? I watched stars on TV and movies and read movie magazines and wondered, from the horrors I read about the lives of these people, would fame and success be worth the price of selling one's soul, giving up a normal family life, one's conscience, one's values, and one's dignity? I didn't have successful people around me to emulate or people with whom to discuss these ideas. My examples were from TV and magazines.

In adolescence as I read the *Bible* and Ralph Waldo Emerson's writings and tried to read Shakespeare, I came across sayings that made me wonder even more what was really true: "As one thinketh in his heart, so he is." "Let God transform you into a new person by changing the way you think. Then you will know what God wants you to do." "Great men are those who see that thoughts rule the World." "There is nothing either good or bad except that thinking makes it so." Did it matter what I thought, how I thought?

Later in life, when I actually deliberately pursued reading more philosophers writings and novelists, I came across other quotes that caused me to wonder about success and how it related to one's thinking. Disraeli said, "Life is too short to be little."

Reading Thoreau's "Walden Pond," I came across this which made me really wonder: did it matter not just what I thought, but what I imagined was possible? I read: "I learned that if one advances confidently in the direction of his dreams, and endeavors to live the life he has imagined, he will meet with a success unexpected in common hours. He will pass an invisible boundary; new, universal, and more liberal laws will begin to establish themselves around and within him; or the old laws will be expanded, and interpreted in his favor in a more liberal sense, and he will live with the license of a higher order of beings."

What he describes has actually been my experience as you will witness in my stories. I've learned to live expecting positive exceptions to be made in my favor, and I suggest you also live with this belief. It makes all the difference in our experience.

True success for most of us means personal prosperity: a lovely place to live, vacations, travel, new things, financial serenity and giving help to others. Success means winning the admiration and trust of others. Success means freedom, freedom from worries, fears, frustrations and failure. Success means self-respect, continually finding more real happiness and satisfaction from life, being able to do more for those you desire to help.

Success is determined not so much by the size of one's brain as it is by the size of one's thinking. I've determined by observation that the size of one's bank accounts, how happy a person is, and the size of one's general satisfaction, is dependent on the size of one's thinking. There is magic in thinking big and thinking positively. We are products of the thinking around us, which is why it is important to surround ourselves with positive people, positive thoughts and with very little exposure to media coverage of so-called current events.

Believe you can succeed and you will, cure yourself of making excuses, overcome your fears, think big, dream creatively, realize you are what you think you are, get in the habit of taking action, set goals, write down your desires. Writing down your thoughts and desires is the best way to clarify them. I've included sheets with the word formulas added for you to duplicate and fill out at the end of the book.

To find out why a thing was created, it is best to ask the Creator. As souls, aspects of God, we made a conscious decision to come to Earth to accomplish and to learn certain things. Remembering what that was gives us our purpose. We did not create ourselves, so there is no way we can tell ourselves why we were created or for what purpose. Since it all begins with God, since we were created by God, the place to look for what we agreed to as our purpose for this life is with God. We can communicate with God though our souls in meditation. It is possible to communicate with our souls and with God, directly. This is something I was not taught while I was involved in religion, but something I learned through desire and desperation. Later, it occurred to me that the church hierarchy didn't teach meditation or direct soul communication because it would put them out of business.

Living without a purpose is not as satisfying as living with a purpose.

We can speculate about our purpose but it is only by communicating with God through our souls that we can discover our origin, our identity, our meaning, our true purpose, our significance and our destiny. The larger, cosmic purpose of our lives fits into a much larger plan called "The Divine Plan of God."

We were all born with free will as a gift from our Creator, and we put forth a great deal of effort to develop it. From the age of two, when we learn to speak, we respond "no" to most everything we are asked and "mine" to almost everything else, because we believed we were separate and that there is not enough of everything for everyone. We see ourselves as separate from God, The Source, The Creator; and, in our desire for control, we ignore inner guidance. We make hearing inner guidance difficult. For many of us, the idea that "we are one with The Creator" was an idea sparked later in life, if at all. My original belief was that God was outside myself on a throne somewhere judging my actions, and certainly not lovingly supporting me in every decision I made. This belief was offered and supported by all the organized religions I experienced in my search for truth.

Seldom have we considered any "will" save our own, unless it was our parent's will, or some authority outside ourselves who held physical power over us, such as physical survival or financial serenity. Even though most of us have been exposed to various versions of the Lord's Prayer all our lives, we have either quasi-sincerely or robotically stated "Thy will be done, on Earth as it is in heaven" without really seriously meaning that we were willing to consider any Higher Will than our own.

The question, "What is the purpose of my life?" seldom comes up until our lives are in a heap at our feet. Or:

The World seems to be crashing down around us.

We have managed to engage ourselves in some major health crisis.

We divorce or separate from a spouse or lover.

We experience the death of someone very close to us.

We lose our job.

We lose our home to creditors, to a fire, is blown away or floods in a storm.

We experience being burglarized or raped.

Our normal reaction would be, "Why is this happening to me?" But we might also think to ask, "Am I doing the 'right' thing?" Or "What is the purpose of my being here on Earth?"

As long as things are still moving, our boat's not rocking too much and the waves are still manageable, we have a tendency to believe we are in control, and "we" are. One of the aforementioned disasters, however, can bring us to our knees, our bed, our death, or our senses.

My story is not that unusual. I created a lot of drama and self-destruction during my first forty years. I began life in a small West Texas town, married early, did not attend college, found out my first husband was gay, divorced early, remarried, had two wonderful children, fell in love with a priest who was my friend's husband, lost my mother through a heart attack, divorced again, took the children to live with me and my new love in Oklahoma City, OK. To cope with the drama I had created to this point, I had taken four Valium per day for fifteen years. At the time of my mother's death I began to question, "What am I doing here? Can I live without the drugs?"

When my lover died of a heart attack in my bed on the fourth day of our new life together, and the children went back to live with their father in Texas, I began to feel that I wasn't doing something "right", or that I had somehow really made God angry. I was excommunicated from the Episcopal Church by the Bishop of West Texas and the Bishop of Oklahoma because my fiancé was an Episcopal priest and it was the only retaliation the men had to show for their displeasure with my choices. I had angered most of my friends by my choice to go with my heart instead of my logic. I now see that they were mostly angry because they did not have nerve enough to go for what they really wanted in life. I was 350 miles from anyone I knew.

I had attended Baptist Sunday school as a child by myself since my family was not religious, switched to Methodism with the first husband and Episcopalism with the second husband. I was very familiar with God and judgment and not at all familiar with the Universal Laws, God's Love, the Spiritual Hierarchy, the Intergalactic Federation, Meditation or the idea that we are all One and the same energy as God, or the concept that the answers lie within us.

Within my aloneness, where I had no roles to play for anyone (no one's daughter, lover, or wife) I was a mother from a distance, my friends had turned against me and I had no job. I began to think a lot about "Why am I here? How did I get here? What should I do next? Who should I work for? What kind of work should I do? Do I want to stay on the earth?" The answer to the last question came back, "Not particularly," which gave me very little enthusiasm for answering the others.

You will note that not once did I ask, "What do I 'desire' to do?" Only the "Shoulds" were there. In getting the divorce and moving to live with my new love, I had done what I "desired" and the price and consequences were overwhelming. My family and friends were angry and convinced I had lost my mind. The church officials added their disapproval.

**Life is meant to be about letting God use us,
not about us using God.**

After moving to Oklahoma, my fiancé's death, and the children moving back to Texas, I went back into banking because it was what I knew. I took a bank teller security class while working at Union bank and met the teacher, whose name is David. When David moved to Houston he convinced the people at Oklahoma University, where he had been teaching, to hire me to teach the class in banks all over Oklahoma. The people at OU never asked for my credentials. I took dancing lessons and met another man named David who was an executive at a local Savings and Loan Association; he convinced his superiors to hire me as a bank consultant to create a teller training program for their tellers. It was a time in history when savings and loans were becoming banks. They did not ask for my credentials.

God does not choose the qualified. God qualifies those who choose to serve.

In August 1982, I finished the bank consulting job with Local Federal. Rather than keep me on as an employee to train their loan tellers to be bankers, as they had promised, I was let go from my job. The same day I was let go from the savings and loan association, I received a call from Peter, a man who periodically came through Oklahoma City on business. He was a very wealthy, older man who lived in California. He had asked me several times to visit him in California and I had always told him I couldn't because I had to work. Well, now I was unemployed and had no excuse. Having been raised to believe men should take care of women, I chose to pursue marriage. I took Peter up on his offer to fly me to California for a ten-day sailing trip on his 35-foot sailboat. He assured me he could sail the boat by himself and that very little would be required of me. Having never been sailing, I imagined lying on the deck reading books while he sailed the boat. I wasn't naive enough to believe there would not be some sex involved, but I was willing. I planned to get Peter to marry me so I would not have to figure out what to do with my life.

I should have suspicions when the air conditioning in the plane failed on the way to California. It was August. I was wearing a white polyester dress, nylon underwear and nylon stockings. When I arrived in California, I was exhausted and soaking wet from sweat. All I wanted was a shower and a nap. Peter seemed excited to see me and our first stop was at a dive shop to get me fitted with a wet suit, because we would be scuba diving off the boat. The wet suit the shop owner offered was still damp from its last user; he offered no talcum powder to make it easier to pull it on. My body was damp and sticky and the suit was damp. I struggled. Cursing under my breath, "This suit was built for a 14-year-old boy with no ass, unlike me." I waddled out to the show room with the suit hanging down twelve inches in the crotch thinking they could obviously see they needed to get me a larger size. The oriental shop owner made an OK sign with his thumb and forefinger and said, "Perfect." I headed back to the dressing room muttering,

"There is no way in hell this is perfect; you must be blind." By the time I got the thing off I was even more exhausted and my arms were aching from the effort.

When we arrived at Peter's townhouse he did not even give me time to take a shower, much less a nap, before he had me across the bed. I stared at the digital clock as he raped me. The man had an erection recovery time of six minutes. I didn't even know this was humanly possible. I wondered if his sexual appetite and endurance were somehow connected to his surviving Auschwitz. When I was finally released to take a shower, I stood in the shower and cried and wondered what I had gotten myself into.

The next morning, before we set sail, Peter took me to The Bodhi Tree, a large bookstore in Los Angeles. He insisted on buying me three books. One on numerology, one on the I Ching and a novel called *A Hundred Years of Solitude* by Gabriel Garcia Marquez. His buying me books on subjects I had no desire to pursue made me think him even more strange than I had the night before, but I was determined to see this vacation through to the end and to attempt to get to know him better.

The ten days on the boat were misery. I was seasick. Peter was constantly yelling at me to move, to get out of the way, to hold this or that. When he wasn't yelling at me, he was attacking my body or cooking Hungarian goulash. I knew quickly I had taken myself to hell, but in the middle of the Pacific I saw no way out. On the tenth day I had had enough. I put on the full scuba diving gear, without putting the air apparatus in my mouth, and jumped into the Pacific to kill myself. During the night a huge yacht had anchored next to us. The men on the yacht recognized that the right kind of bubbles weren't coming up where I had entered the water and one jumped in to rescue me. Peter expressed his disappointment in me and we headed back into the harbor.

After unsuccessfully attempting to kill myself, I was ready to give up. The day that I left Texas to move to Oklahoma with Edward, the priest, I went to a Walden's bookstore and bought a book to read aloud to him in the moving van. I did not know the book was metaphysical and I did not even know that word. The name of the book is *Illusions* by Richard Bach. I read the book to Edward and we both loved it. Years later, the day I returned from California, I noticed it lying on the coffee table with the back cover turned up. I picked it up and read:

"Here is a test to find whether your mission on Earth is finished: If you're alive it isn't."

I took the message seriously. I had always been religious, but never really expected God to speak to me personally. I had never totally turned my life over to God because the people I had witnessed in the church who did this went to Africa or somewhere equally foreign to be a missionary and I knew for sure I didn't want to be a missionary or go to a foreign country. That day I deliberately told God, "I turn my life over to you. If you will just talk to me I will go anywhere, do anything, and say anything you want."

I expected a big Charlton Hesston kind of voice to respond, but nothing happened. No booming voice said, "I hear you" or "go to Africa" or anything else. I decided to go to a book store and look in the Self-Help section to see if anyone had written a book on how to find your life's purpose. As I entered a neighborhood B. Dalton's book store, I walked past the Occult Sciences section. I would have normally avoided anything occult or psychic to the extent that I would have walked around this section of the store because of my inherited and well ingrained beliefs. Psychic and occult practices were religiously taught to be of the devil. This day my depression was so great I forgot my precautions and prejudices and walked right by the Occult Science section. As I passed, a book titled Psychic Energy by Joseph Weed fell off the shelf onto the floor directly in front of me. Since I was aware that I had in no way jarred or touched the shelf, I was puzzled by the event. I picked up the book and examined the cover. I was not positively impressed by the book. It was a paperback book printed on newsprint paper and the cover was not attractive, printed in red, white and purple and the print was crooked. Everything about the book offended my Librarian sense of beauty and order. I read the back of the book:

PSYCHIC ENERGY
How to Change Desires Into Realities by Joseph Weed

> "This is a valuable book, a precious book which you will want to keep near you and read again and again. It lifts the veil of mystery and superstition that has for too long shrouded the puzzling phenomena so often seen today. In truth, there are no deviations from natural law. Everything that happens, no matter how exotic it may seem, can be explained and understood. Many of these so-called 'wild talents' are described herein and their functions analyzed in simple, non-technical language.
>
> Habitually, we all think in terms of the visible, the material. Yet man is not an animal and he cannot live like one and be happy.

On the other hand, neither is he a god - and any attempt to deify his higher nature at the expense of his Human heritage is equally doomed to fail. A balance is necessary, and the suggestions given herein will guide you to the attainment of proper harmonium.

In this book you will find information that will surprise and often amaze you. For example..."

I placed the book back on the shelf and proceeded to the Self-Help, Psychology, Religion, and Philosophy sections. I read cover after cover and found nothing that spoke directly to the issue of finding my life purpose. Disappointed and even more depressed, I proceeded to leave the store. As I once again passed the Occult section, I glanced toward the shelf where I had replaced the *Psychic Energy* book. To my amazement the book was now lit up. A white glowing light was emanating from and circling the book.

Many thoughts went through my mind. "I am now having a nervous breakdown. I've earned it and this light is proof. Objects don't just fall off shelves and objects don't just light up." Curiosity overcoming logic, I purchased the book and took it home. Still very skeptical, I seated myself on the couch with the book between my hands and said a prayer before I opened it. "If this book is of God I will open it to one page and there will be a message from God." I opened the book in the center and read:

INSTRUCTIONS FOR INSPIRED WRITING

"If you would like to experiment with inspired writing follow these instructions.
1. "Always take a bath before any automatic writing session. This is not only to cleanse yourself physically of impurities that may be clinging to you but it is also symbolical of a spiritual cleansing which should take place before exposing yourself to any foreign influence.
2. "Sit at a desk or table where you will not be disturbed and compose yourself.
3. "When you are completely relaxed physically, emotionally and clear mentally, take three deep breaths, letting each one out quite slowly.
4. "Then take pen or pencil in your hand, place it on the top line of the blank pad before you, see that your arm is comfortable and relax.

"You may get a response the first time but more than likely not. So try again and repeat the preparation here outlined each time. If after a serious attempt, on five different occasions, you get no result, set the idea aside temporarily and try it again in a year when you and conditions about you will have changed.

"If your hand starts to write, it may turn out serious material or it may write nonsense. If the latter, stop immediately and try again another time, making sure you prepare yourself most carefully. Foolish, childish or confused writing is evidence of a poor connection (so to speak) or contact with a low grade personality. If this occurs, try the next time to raise the level of your consciousness by clearing your mind of low-grade thoughts and impulses. Usually you can establish a satisfactory mood by prayer, or by reading a passage from the *Bible* or another inspirational work.

"When you get a serious response, do not hesitate to ask aloud 'Who is this?' You will, as a rule, get a completely candid answer to this and to any other legitimate question that may occur to you. Once you have learned how to relax your hand and arm and have caught on to the proper "don't care" attitude, interesting results should ensue. Automatic writing is not something new, or strange, or so very different. Many people practice it and there are literally thousands of books, documents and reports written this way that are available for examination."

THIS INFORMATION WAS NOT IN THE BOOK, BUT I HAVE SINCE LEARNED THAT IF YOU CHOOSE TO DO THIS MEDITATION, I RECOMMEND YOU FIRST SEAL THE ROOM IN WHICH YOU ARE MEDITATING BY SAYING: "I DELIBERATELY SEAL THIS ROOM ON THE NORTH, SOUTH, EAST AND WEST; I SEAL THE CEILING AND THE FLOOR AGAINST ANY NEGATIVE ENERGY OR ENTITY. I ASK TO COMMUNICATE ONLY WITH MY OWN SOUL OR GOD."

I finished reading the two pages, laid the book aside and made a conscious decision to try this foreign-to-me form of communication since I had asked for direct communication. I took a shower, dressed in a robe, took the phone off the hook, gathered pencil and legal pad, lit a white candle, sat on the couch with my back straight, bare feet on the floor and recited the Lord's Prayer. I began to breathe deeply, becoming aware of my breath as I exhaled slowly.

My conscious mind or, as I later learned, my left brain, my ego, pointed out to me, "This is really dumb. This is the dumbest thing you've ever done.

This is not going to work. You should be out looking for a job not sitting here doing such a weird thing. At least put the phone back on the hook so it can ring and on, and on, and on...." I tried to ignore my doubts and continued to breathe deeply and waited, wishing my hand would begin to move. After what seemed like about ten minutes I had another set of words in my mind on the right side of my head separate from the objections and yet still in my own voice:

"Through this pen will come...Through this pen will come... Through this pen will come...Through this pen will come..."

Since I was expecting the writing to be automatic I just kept listening. I'm not a very patient person so after the fourth repetition I asked mentally, "Will come what?"

"The words you need..."

At this reply I began to realize I was to write down what was coming into my head instead of my hand moving automatically, more like taking dictation, inspired but not automatic writing. The words continued:

September 30, 1982
"Through this pen will come the words you need to express the feelings of the world and how you feel about them. I want you to now relax, accept, identify and examine your motives for this experiment. This day has been given for your use. It is a free gift. You may, however, be placing a price that I have not required. Try accepting my gift without reservation or reluctance. Test this program for thirty days. I will make manifest to you My will for your life and can guarantee you will be amazed at how closely it will parallel your own true desires. Forget all else that troubles you. Choose to accept each new assignment as it appears before you in whatever form it takes, whether a person to be entertained, a task to be accomplished, a chore to be done or a piece of creativity for which you will be given the strength, knowledge, ability and insight to reach a level of awareness you never dreamed imaginable.

"Take this opportunity to reflect...What do you really desire to do? Where do you really desire to be?

"Try this method of putting yourself in contact with the answers to these questions by listening to a pattern of speech coming from your unconscious awareness. If the phone rings, answer with the attitude that you are willing to comfort, be with, or respond to the person on the other end. Create an atmosphere of acceptance for

yourself, your faults and your imagined short comings. With my power you have the ability to create, activate and accomplish many marvelous things. I choose you as my instrument of peace to be used by Me in a World that truly needs peace. I will activate in you an energy supply unequaled by any other, my energy, which I give to you this day as a free gift to be accepted or rejected as you choose. I am willing to see you as an equal to me, ready to respond at a moment's notice to the needs of others and, in so doing, be aware that you are not only accomplishing my goals but your own. Now, take your pen and express the feelings I give you in My words and I will reward you with My grace. Try as you will with my love and you will succeed beyond your dreams.

"I have a plan for Our life in you. Give it a chance to materialize and I will reward your efforts by being near you to comfort, guide and direct these efforts in the way for which I have created you to flow.

"This is not a test of endurance, but a test of faith, you cannot fail, and you can only stop to begin again. When you feel yourself take control of your life - STOP - examine your results. Do they agree with what you truly desire to do with your life? If not, pause, listen and redirect your thinking to Me and to my words as I give them to you. You are My child and I care what happens to you in this life. I expect you to care what happens, too. This is your life, freely given by Me: I need your life to accomplish My plan. I am willing to assist in any situation you desire my help. Because you are willing, I can use you for my projection into the World at the Human level. Take My hand as I lead you today and don't fear the outcome; just trust the process that takes us there. We can accomplish things together that cannot be accomplished in any other way.

"Support for your efforts will be made available through an unexpected source and should not be a concern for you at this time.

"Redo your work when you feel you have not pleased yourself, because you are aware of the need for quality in Our approach.

"Accept the things I send as gifts, not questioning why they should be yours. You deserve My love. It is freely given to you as you express it to others. I will create the material needs you have to be fulfilled.

"Right at this moment there is a need that I will make you aware of shortly, to be accomplished as quickly as possible. Now replace the telephone receiver and wait."

Seven pages later I heard no more words and stopped writing to read what had been written.

"My motives?" I felt my only motive was desperation to have answers about my purpose for being.

"**Test this method for thirty days.**" That seemed fair. I apparently could reserve judgment. I had been questioning my sanity, but I knew I would not personally set myself up to do anything for thirty days. This was the only part of the message I knew I didn't make up.

"**I will make manifest to you My will for your life and can guarantee you will be amazed at how closely it will parallel your own desires.**" This line gave me hope that I would not be sent to Africa to be a missionary.

"**Choose to accept each new assignment as it appears before you in whatever form it takes, whether a person to be entertained, a task to be accomplished, a chore to be done or a piece of creativity for which you will be given the strength, knowledge, ability and insight to reach a level of awareness you never dreamed imaginable.**" Somehow, put into those terms, it didn't feel as if I would be asked to do anything weird or anything that I could not do with the help that was seemingly being offered.

I replaced the phone receiver in its cradle and was startled when it rang immediately. The call was from an elderly neighbor who needed a ride to the doctor's office. "**If the phone rings, answer with the attitude that you are willing to comfort, be with or respond to the person on the other end.**" I agreed to chauffeur my neighbor to the doctor. As you can imagine, I was in a state of awe and disbelief from my writing experience.

"**What do you really desire to do? Where do you really desire to be?**" This was more difficult for me to define. I had experienced a very limited amount of the World, how could I know what I desired? I wanted to shout again, "If I'd known what I desired I wouldn't be asking you!" More questions didn't seem like a good answer to my original question.

When I returned from my chauffeuring I tried to make a list of what I desired to do:

1. I desire to do something creative. (Thinking but not writing: not count other people's money all day.)

2. I desire to do something that helps people to communicate. (Thinking but not writing: this seemed like the biggest problem in the World to me.)

3. I desire to work at home, in case my children want to come back to live with me.

4. I desire to do something I can't be fired from. (Termination of

employment once in a lifetime is more than enough.)

5. I desire to teach adults.

6. I desire to help people to self-actualize. (I wasn't sure exactly how, but I did know I wanted to learn to become all I could be and to do what I had come to Earth to experience and to share that with others. I'd read one book about self-actualization given to me by a chiropractor I had met at a singles meeting called *The Magic of Self-Actualization* by Dr. R. C. Schafer.

(If I'm honest, I was trying to impress God that I knew such a big word.)

I remembered the book said: "Every life exists for the purpose of making a meaningful contribution. Without a purpose that is deeply enjoyed, it is not a life, only an existence. To increase pleasure and reduce the time necessary to achieve the goals of our choice is a primary concern for those of us who are non-technical people, who find ourselves in a highly technical society. To meet this end, we frequently spend huge sums on trinkets, gadgets, and a multitude of status symbols only to find that any satisfaction we derive is fleeting. Then somebody suddenly decides that the solution to all ills is to move to a new neighborhood, a new job, a new membership in some organization, or even select a new mate. The result, however, is only old problems in new places. The answer cannot be found in things and places, only in understanding ourselves and Human nature."

I laid the brief list beside my bed and slept soundly for eleven hours.

"Nothing in this World is as powerful as an idea whose time has come."
— **Victor Hugo**

The following morning after my shower I repeated the meditation from the day before. The words began almost immediately.

October 1, 1982
"You will now be an artist. Buy a set of watercolors and parchment paper. You will start a greeting card company called bj originals, inc. Use all lower case letters for your name and no periods. Fold the parchment paper in thirds and paint on the front section. In the middle section you will do calligraphy of the messages I will give you. The cards will sell for $2.00."

I immediately began to argue. "I don't know how to paint. I'm not an artist. I have no education in art. I think you have the wrong person. By creative I meant not boring; I didn't mean I have any talent. I meant I didn't want to count other people's money all day or work in a factory doing something repetitious. I only know how to do the calligraphy because I took six nights of calligraphy lessons at a Methodist Church before I left Texas. I know even less about creating a business or marketing greeting cards. And I only have $105.00 left in the World." The words continued as if I was not arguing. The message assured me that I could paint, that all I needed to do was to buy watercolors, brushes and a book called *Drawing on the Right Side of the Brain* by Betty Edwards. I was asked to do the exercises in the book and was told in a meditative state I would be able to allow the paintings to happen through me. I had $105.00 in the World. The next message was not welcomed.

"Take $100.00 of the $105.00 and open a business account in the name of bj originals, Inc. Notify the state that you can no longer accept unemployment compensation for you are now self-employed."

This advice really made me wonder if this was God. I thought God would be smart enough to know that service charges for a bank account would eat up the money before I had a chance to spend it. I thought I knew more about banking and money than God apparently did.

You can imagine how well I took that suggestion! The advice did not compute to my left brain, my Third dimensional reality. First I explained to the source of the message that it obviously did not understand much about banking and explained that one does not open two checking accounts when one only has such a small amount of money because the bank service charges would eat up what was there. I further explained that I wasn't yet making any money being self-employed. I agreed that when I was making money I would quit accepting the unemployment. Every day for six days the message was identical. I now see that the majority of lessons I have had to learn in this life have been in the area of money and relationships, particularly male/female relationships. Therefore, this has been where my tests of faith or, of necessity, my leaps of faith have been.

I somehow came to the conclusion that I must either quit meditating and listening to the advice or go with the advice. I gave up the unemployment and opened the bank account. I bought the parchment paper, watercolors, calligraphy pens, ink, envelopes, and the book *Drawing on the Right Side of the Brain*. I began to do the exercises in the book and found to my surprise that I was able to sketch and able to do an oriental form of brush work. From the end of the brush would come a flower, with a butterfly suspended over the flower. When you do something you don't know how to do, it is fun to watch yourself do it.

After I followed the suggestions, money began to come. I received a check for $50.00 for my birthday from my father who never before had sent me money or acknowledged my birthday since my Mother's death. I received an insurance refund and then an IRS refund from two years prior. I began to sell the cards to my friends.

Through the years, after I took Silva Mind Control training, I modified the meditation and this is the one I use now, which I have found to be very effective.

bj's MORNING MEDITATION

I deliberately seal this room on the north, south, east and west, the ceiling and the floor against any negative energy or entity. I ground myself into the magnetic energy at the core of the Earth to be stable and to strengthen the iron in my blood.

I call forth the blue light of protection for myself, Muffin, my home, car and my family. I ask to extend this protective bubble of blue light of protection from Guthrie to Norman and from Shawnee to El Reno; protection from high damaging wind, excessive rain, flooding, hail, excessive snow and ice, fire, tornadoes, earthquakes, theft, terrorism and violence.

I open my heart in gratitude for my body, my Oversoul, my I Am Presence, my Holy Christ self, the Earth, all the animals, plants, minerals, water, fire, air and ethers, the Spiritual Hierarchy, the Intergalactic Federation, all of the Angelic Realm, the Planetary Logos, the Solar Logos, the Sun and the Moon, the Creator God of all Universes.

I ask for the Violet Flame of Transmutation to flow through the cells of my body, my conscious and sub-conscious minds to remove all limiting beliefs, doubts, fears, judgments, negativity, jealousy and anger. I ask that all the cells of my body be healed and transformed to perfection. I ask my body intelligence to normalize the functions of my glands to produce exactly the amount my body needs, no more and no less. I ask that my body be polarized perfectly between the North and South Poles. I ask that all the static electricity be dissipated, dissipated, dissipated from my brain and body.

I call forth the blue light of protection for myself, my home, my car and my pets, protection from accidents, damaging wind, excessive rain, flooding, hail, tornadoes, earthquakes, volcanic eruptions, vandalism, theft and terrorism.

I send a beam of energy from my heart, through my high heart and my mid-brain and into all levels of my Oversoul, my I AM Presence, my Holy Christ self, and into the Ascended Master's octave of Light.

I give my I AM Presence and Holy Christ Self dominion over my body, my thoughts, emotions and actions. I take a deep breath, hold it at the point of my mid-brain and count 3, 3, 3 and exhale. I take another deep breath, hold it at the mid-brain and count 2, 2, 2 and exhale. I take another deep breath, hold it at the mid-brain and count 1, 1, 1 and exhale. I count backward from 10 to one and sit quietly and wait for the telepathic messages from my soul about what is the next single thing for me to do or know for me to be in a state of Divine Grace? Then I wait for the response from my soul.

2.

Find the Positive by Looking at the Negative

Begin by looking at what you have in your life you don't want, don't like or are dissatisfied with. I have found that sometimes beginning with looking at what is in my life that I don't want makes it easier for me to be clear about what I desire to have to replace what's currently in my life.

Take these statements and turn them around into positive affirmations, but watch the way you word your affirmations. You can trip yourself up, thinking you've made a positive statement when you haven't. Remember always that the sub-conscious and the soul take our beliefs and statements literally.

NEGATIVE "I WANT'S"

I don't want to get a ticket.
I don't want to be ripped off.
I don't want my child to get hurt.
I don't want to fail the test.
I don't want to be sick.
I don't want to become helpless when I get older.
I don't want my car to break down.
I don't want to live like this.
I don't want to have to pay so many taxes.
I don't want to make a mistake
I hate war.

It is important to be in favor of what you do want and not against anything. What you are against you give energy to whether it is against drugs, drunk drivers, war, killing seals or whales, rain forest destruction, aids, or against homelessness and hunger.

Pay attention to when you are saying "I want" but vibrating "I don't want."

I want out of this relationship.

I want a job that pays better.

I want the government out of my life

I want to get out of debt.

In these thoughts you are still thinking more about what you don't want than what you do want even if you are saying "I want."

Intention is a much better choice than "I want or I need." The soul and the sub-conscious take our statements literally. If we say "I want" the soul and sub-conscious believe we desire to stay in a state of wanting. If we say "I need" the soul and sub-conscious believe we desire to stay in a state of needing.

It is far more productive to say " I desire, intend, deserve and now gratefully receive." This fulfills the points it takes to manifest. You have desire, belief, expectancy, willingness to receive and gratitude.

Our job is to state the desires in writing as we would if we were filling out a purchase order. We then need to become aware of insights, intuitions and messages coming from our soul. Once we've put the order out into the Universe, it is <u>not</u> our job to figure out the "how" a thing can happen. In actuality, we are not smart enough or creative enough to think up the "how." Normally, Humans will limit God by believing there are only a few ways a thing can happen. These usually involve more overtime, inheritance or winning the lottery. If we release the "how" to the Universe and pay attention to the intuition by only asking our soul:

What is the next single thing for me to do or know, for me to be in a state of divine grace?

And release the request with the statement:

I now accept this or something better through the grace of God and to the highest good of all concerned.

We have given permission for the desire to be fulfilled in whatever manner God chooses and whatever manner serves the highest good; we've agreed through saying "now accept" in having what we ask for now; and we've agreed to accept whatever messenger God chooses to use to bring us our good.

It is important <u>not</u> to look to your job, social security, your parents, your spouse or retirement income as the source of your supply. If you do, you limit the number of directions that can be used by God to get your good to you. It is important to see your job or your daily efforts as your contribution to the Universe, not as a direct exchange for a certain payment amount.

I desire joy to radiate through my heart at all times.
I desire my whole family to feel joy.
I desire to feel that everything is always as it should be.
I desire an increased sense of freedom
I desire to remember that I always have choices.
I intend to see more choices.
I intend to trust that all is well in the world.
I intend to learn deliberate co-creating.
I intend to learn to be a better energy manager.
I intend to become aware of my resistances.
I intend to be constantly aware of my true feelings.
I intend to enjoy my life to the fullest.
I intend to have more and more fun and experience more and more peace.
I intend to experience health, stamina and muscle strength.
I intend to daily have a closer connection with my Source.

Many of us were raised with sayings that no longer serve us:
That's life, accept it.
That's just the way things are.
Life is not fair, don't expect it.
You can't fight City Hall.
Stop knocking your head against a brick wall.
That's just the way of the World.
There is no free lunch.
Within every life a little rain must fall.
Learn to take life on its terms.
Get your head out of the clouds.
Wise up and face reality.
In my case it was: Get that book out of your face and quit trying to act

above your raising.

    Watch what you say habitually. Things like:
I feel like I've been run over by a truck.
What she did just makes me sick.
I'm exhausted.
I'm dead tired.
My fate is up to the judge.
I have a headache, backache, stomachache.
I'm afraid I'm catching a cold.
I always experience hay fever at this time of year.
I'm afraid this is not going to work out.
I don't see how this situation could possibly change.
Sales are down because the economy is bad right now.
Of course this is happening to me; I'm getting old.
As long as the Republicans are in power...

ALWAYS EXPECT THE UNIVERSE TO MAKE POSITIVE EXCEPTIONS IN YOUR FAVOR.

    We manifest from how we are feeling, thinking and expressing ourselves. We must stay conscious and correct ourselves. How we are feeling affects our vibrations. The higher our vibrations, the clearer intention and image we hold, the faster the manifestation happens.
    It feels strong to me to precede my request with:

**I desire, intend, and now gratefully receive or
I desire, intend, and now gratefully accept.**

    Gratitude for what the Universe has already granted us is the most important step in manifestation. Keep a gratitude journal in which you write daily at least five things for which you are grateful.

3.

How to Gain Deliberate Control of Your Life Understanding The Universal Law Of Attraction

That which is vibrationally like unto itself is magnetized to itself. You get what you think about whether you want it or not.

There are Universal Laws that affect everything in the Universe, the physical and the non-physical. These Laws are in effect and working whether we believe in them, understand them, or not. They are eternal and operating everywhere simultaneously. We can deliberately use this Law and create what we desire, or we can ignore it and create by default. Once you understand that all people, circumstances and events are invited into your experience by you, through your thought, you can begin to change your life by changing your thoughts. Trust me, when I first heard this information, I thought it to be so much BS. I did not believe what was happening to me was in any way connected to how I thought or the beliefs I held.

    Being told that I invited unwanted things into my experience through my attention to them sounded ridiculous. How could I possibly be in control of what was happening to me? I didn't have control of all these other people who were causing me to feel afraid, inadequate and undesirable. This had to be their fault. I was totally committed to being concerned about what other people thought and expected of me. I had been well- taught by my mother that to worry meant you cared about the person you were worrying about.

One of the first books I read in my progression was Terry Cole-Whitaker's *What You Think of Me Is None of My Business*. I was horrified that I allowed <u>what I thought other people thought of me</u> to control so much of my behavior. It took me quite a while to figure out they weren't usually thinking about me at all and that most of the expectations I placed upon myself came from what I projected that they might be thinking or might be expecting. Then there was Napoleon Hill's *Think and Grow Rich*. I read it several times and still wasn't convinced that what I thought was going to make any difference in what happened in my life. Then I came across Florence Scovel Shinn's *The Game of Life*. The language bothered me, and all the Bible references bothered me, but the simplicity and energy of what she had to say stuck with me. Her examples were outdated, but I decided to try writing down a few of my desires, just in case what she was saying was real. As soon as I began to write down my desires, and to use a few affirmations, things began to change. I didn't stick with it, because actually it frightened me to see that what I was writing and what I was thinking actually began to happen. The idea that I could be that powerful was scary.

A little later, after I had made direct connection to my soul, I came in contact with Sarah Ban Breathnach's *Simple Abundance*. This book changed my life. I got serious about creating a more beautiful, simple, abundant life. My soul explained that one of my missions in coming to Earth was to demonstrate manifestation and to teach manifestation. Sarah's book encouraged me to start a gratitude journal for writing down what I was grateful for on a daily basis. Her affirmations were in simple language that I could relate to. I began to make a manifestation book and posters with cut out pictures of things I desired to attract into my life. More positive things began to happen. This time I didn't feel as much fear. If this was my mission, I figured I'd better keep going, even if it scared me. I gave up being homeless and created a home; I attracted a loving relationship. I got out of debt. I began to accept I AM an artist, writer and teacher.

I learned <u>not</u> to use words like want and need, since my sub-conscious mind and my soul were always listening to my thoughts and taking me literally. I understood that to use these words made my soul and sub-conscious mind think I wanted to stay in a state of wanting and needing, rather than having and accepting. I learned to listen to what I was thinking. Monitoring my thoughts, I caught myself limiting what could happen by what had happened in the past. I had to learn to overcome believing that if something was going to happen, it was completely up to me to <u>make</u> it happen.

In the first message I received from my soul, I was told that my job would be to state in writing my "true heart's desires." In the beginning, I didn't know what I desired. I had only ever thought in terms, what do I need to survive. It was suggested that I breathe into my heart and ask myself over and over, "What is my true heart's desire?" I did this until the truth began to surface. I had so successfully hidden my desires behind belief in limitation, undeservedness, doubt, fear and disbelief that it took a while for me to admit the truth to myself and to my soul. I would suggest now that if you don't know what you desire, or if you think you don't desire anything more than what you already have, that you might begin to ask to have your desires revealed to you by your soul. The desires of our heart are also the desires of our soul. When you do this, the soul will begin to put ideas in your mind or bring you in contact with things that interest or intrigue you.

We didn't come to Earth to survive; we came to thrive. It does not serve the World for us to play at being small. We are miraculous creations of God. Our purpose is to allow the soul that created us to do through us. Our job is to remember we are not the body. We are the spirit that inhabits the body. The soul created the body for its use in this dimension. Ask to know your purpose, the purpose for which the soul created the body. Ask for what is yours by divine right and under grace, in a perfect way.

Things are attracted to us by our emotions, thoughts, vibrations and actions. We have a responsibility to keep our vibrations as high as possible. What will come to us will match our vibration. Be sure to raise the vibrations of your food, drink, supplements and medications higher than the vibration of your body by putting your hands around it and mentally stating the request, "I now raise the vibration of this higher than the vibration of my body." Hanging out with people who choose to remain stagnant, choose to think and expect negativity, and does not serve us or our souls. We have a responsibility to avoid exposing ourselves to the negativity of the media. This does not mean we have our head in the sand. It means that if something happening in the World is our responsibility to know, our soul will make sure the information reaches us. The newscasters and weather reporters are interested in drama, ratings and creating excitement. We have a responsibility to be at peace, to focus on peace, beauty, harmony and love. We create what we think about. We receive the essence of what we think about.

We have a responsibility to create our own world and to let others choose their own World. This is what it means to be in the World, but not of the World. We cannot send out thoughts of peace and love while exposing ourselves to images of disaster and mayhem.

It is extremely important for us to pay close attention to our emotions. Our emotions are an indicator of whether we are focusing on things we desire or things we don't desire. They are signals from the soul as to whether we are moving toward or away from our goals.

How you see yourself and how you define you is important. The truth of who we are is, "I AM God operating through my personality for the benefit of Earth, all species of life on the Earth and beyond. This is the truth of who I AM." When we think of ourselves in any other way we are limiting the truth and not allowing the soul access to the body and our thoughts. To define ourselves by our job title, our relationships, our nationality, our religious affiliation or any role we play is an error. We are not our roles and we are not our bodies. We are spirits here to have the Human experience. We are not Humans attempting to become spiritual. We are spirits attempting to be Human.

When we worry, we are misusing our creative ability. We are working to manifest what we don't desire. We get what we fear and what we worry about. It takes the same amount of energy and focus to think about what you desire instead of worrying about what might happen. When we think about what we lack, we create more lack. When we think about disease or the possibility of having an accident, we invite it into our lives. The more you think about illness, talk about illness, worry about illness and fear illness, the more you attract illness. I desire to remain healthy and to have strength and vitality.

When you think of someone as a pain in your neck or a pain in your ass, you can give yourself a pain in that area of your body. When we are stiff-necked, stubborn about not being willing to change or to see another person's view, we can also create a stiff neck for ourselves physically. When we are afraid to move forward in our lives, we will usually create problems in our hips or knees. When we are afraid to reach for what we desire it usually shows up in our hands, wrists and shoulders. When we don't stand up for ourselves, often the legs will begin to fail us. Being around someone who irritates us usually causes us to have a sinus infection. Holding onto irritation about anything will cause an irritation in our bodies. There is usually a sub-conscious reason we would choose to be ill or disabled in some way. I have several friends who have decided they don't want to challenge themselves to work for a living so they have created disabilities severe enough to qualify for Social Security disability.

Some of the affirmations about health that I use:

I desire, intend, claim, accept and am now grateful to receive perfect health for myself and my family.

My body is free of all diseases, fungi, pain, viruses and misqualified cells.

The miraculous healing Cosmic Power is now flowing through me and permeating every atom and cell of my body.

Every cell and organ of my body is now complete and perfect and functions according to Divine Law.

God is hearing and seeing through me; my eyesight and hearing are perfect now.

My heart is strong and works perfectly to carry blood and oxygen to every cell of my body.

My body is radiant, healthy, beautiful and strong.

My hair is thick and easy to manage and my nails are strong.

I give thanks for the continuous healing that is taking place in my body, mind, spirit and memory.

My teeth and gums are strong and healthy now.

My body releases toxins and waste materials daily, easily and painessly.

My skin is soft, firm and retains its elasticity.

The energy of God, in and through me, forever cleanses, heals and renews every organ and every atom in my body after the pattern of perfection.

My heart is a living center through which the Love of God flows to bless me and all others I encounter. I AM a birthless, ageless, deathless Spirit.

I intend joyous survival, joyous creating, and harmony.

I intend to eat well and to be comfortable in my body.

I AM surrounded by people with whom I AM harmonious.

I AM erasing every pattern of disease in my cells and my sub-conscious mind, while restoring the pattern of perfect health.

I manifest my I AM Presence through this body now.

I AM Spirit; perfect, holy, harmonious. I constantly manifest my true authentic self through this body.

God in me is infinite wisdom; I always know just what to do.

The Cosmic Healing Power, which made my body and all its organs, knows all the processes and functions of my body and the miraculous Healing Power is permeating every atom of my being, making me whole and perfect. All my organs are God's ideas and, through the power of the Almighty, they are all functioning perfectly now.

Spirit, Divine Life and energy flow freely to every part of my being, cleansing, revitalizing and restoring me to Perfect Health.

I now surrender every personal doubt, fear, or hard feeling that might retard the perfect flow of life through me. There is no obstruction in my mind, my veins, or my affairs. I AM harmonious, peaceful, free and courageous.

The Laws of Harmony, Grace, Beauty and Balance are governing my life now.

I AM filled with peace, strength, power and decision of Spirit. I AM complete and perfect now. My body is pure spiritual substance and as such it is perfect and harmonious.

It is important that the affirmations you choose to use are in words that you would use and express what you desire your sub-conscious to believe.

Our sub-conscious and our souls do not understand humor. When we say things as a jest, the sub-conscious takes us literally. When someone asks you how you feel and you respond, "I feel like I've been run over by a Mack truck," we are inviting just that sort of experience. One I hear people using now a lot is, "He threw me under the bus." Don't assume that because some television program says it is cold and flu season that you need to accept that you will get the flu or will automatically get a cold. You get what you expect. You get what you focus upon. You get what you affirm. Be very careful what you say after the expression "I AM." Make an effort not to use such terms as, "Give me a break" or "that breaks my heart."

Every thought we think has creative potential. Every thought we think while feeling strong emotion is even more likely to happen quickly. We have a tendency to affirm something positive and immediately discount the thought by thinking it isn't possible since you can't figure out how it would happen. The "how" is God's job, your soul's job. Being clear about what you desire and writing it down is your job. Replace in your vocabulary the words desire and accept for the words want and need.

When you write out your desires, I have found it to be helpful to use the phrase: I desire, intend, deserve and now gratefully accept _____ _____. Describe your desire to the best of your ability in detail. This phrase includes all the components of manifestation; desire, intention, belief, expectation or anticipation, present tense and gratitude. At the bottom of each page of desire descriptions I always write: "I now accept this or something better through the grace of God and to the highest good of all concerned." I have learned that the soul is always thinking bigger than I seem to be able to imagine and this clause gives them permission to give me something even better than I have been able to imagine.

When you are feeling down or depressed, make an effort to think a thought that is a bit more uplifting than what you are currently feeling and move to that vibrationally. Usually it helps to think of something for which you can feel grateful. It is difficult to move directly from depression to joy, but you can move gradually from depression to feeling a bit more optimistic, a bit more grateful. Then to move from that thought up to something a bit more hopeful and on and on until you get yourself up off the couch and once again functioning. Don't attempt to go emotionally from zero to sixty in one moment. It won't work.

When you are feeling disappointment, it is a clear indication that what you are focusing on is not truly what you desire to experience, and it is usually an indication you have put someone else in control of your happiness or your future. Usually when I feel disappointed I can look back and see that I did not clearly project the outcome I truly desired to experience.

The Universe, your sub-conscious and your soul do not distinguish between what you see and what you imagine. This is why our imagination is one of our greatest gifts. If we can imagine it, the World and the Universe will work with us to create it. Whether the imagining is positive or negative is not censored by the Universe or your soul. This is why what we really want, we get, and why what we really don't want, we also get. This is why it is important to make what you truly desire to be your most dominant thought and vibration. Thought and emotion are the stuff that is the vehicle through which all things are attracted or created. Guide your thoughts in the direction of things that feel better and better.

To desire a wonderful life is not selfish. We desire for others what we also desire for ourselves. We can only assist those in other countries who are suffering by visualizing them fed, clothed, housed and well. The positive energy we send with these visions can cause miracles of change to happen in their lives. Imagine them in a better situation, successful and happy. The greatest gift you can give another is the gift of your expectation of their success.

When you find yourself in the midst of a painful situation, or with a seemingly insurmountable problem, ask your soul for a solution, not an answer or a fix. An answer then has to be figured out by your mind, a fix will surely need to be fixed again, but a solution is a method to dissolve the situation. Turn your undivided attention to the successful resolution of the situation, not focusing on the situation as it appears.

Allowing others their right to be how they are is one of our most difficult challenges, especially when we think we know what would help them or solve their situation. We are here to be examples of demonstration of good in our lives. People will not come and ask us how to suffer. They have that figured out, but if our lives look like fun, healthy, interesting, successful lives, people will ask us how we did it. Then we can share what we know of the Law of Attraction. People only learn by example.

Humans have a tendency to only believe what they have seen or previously experienced. The mass consciousness belief is that to become wealthy one must win the lottery, marry rich, inherit wealth or work really hard. Once I got the example that God had created 6000 varieties of just begonias, it occurred to me that She was probably capable of thinking of more than four ways to solve any problem I could create. Sometimes you can envision how a thing can happen, but more often than not when we try to do this we are getting in the way or limiting how it could happen. Visioning is good, but only if we envision the end result, not the method of how to get there. Leave the how to the soul or the Universe; focus only on the desired end result and ask continually, "What is the next single thing for me to do or know for me to be in a state of divine grace?" After you ask the question, be prepared to do what you feel intuitively is your next step. My experience is that it is not useful for me to try to figure out how the next step I intuit that is mine to do has to do with me getting the end result I desire. In my experience of working with the soul and God, I'm pretty sure the straight line method of being the fastest way to reach a goal has not occurred to the soul. They are always more interested in the people I will meet along the way than in efficiency or expediency.

I have recently learned the power of action in the direction of my desire. When we moved into the Center, I had large, long, tiered flower beds built all across the back yard. I must have thought I would be 40 forever when I did such an expanse of flower beds. Keeping weeds and grass out of them became a real issue. I noticed that I enjoyed container gardening much more than planting in the flower beds themselves. I began to envision having them cleared out and filled with landscaping fabric and mulch and then putting containers of flowers on top of the mulch. My action in that direction was to purchase the supplies. A few days later, a couple of the ladies in the Thursday night class asked me what I intended to do with all the supplies I had piled on the deck. I explained my vision and they said they would love to help, which they did, and it now looks exactly like my vision.

My grandson gave me two bird feeders last year which he painted lavender, my favorite color. I have many other bird feeders in the yard which were not attractive. Last week I decided to buy paint and paint them all lavender. I went to the store to get a can of paint and a brush, rather than cans of spray paint, because in Oklahoma we have very few windless days. I waited in the department for someone to come to mix the paint for me and no one came. I walked around and discovered six cans of purple spray paint on sale. No other color was on sale. I took it as a sign that I would be able to spray them and bought the cans. The next morning I woke up to one of the few still days in Oklahoma and sprayed them all, and they look lovely.

When I was still homeless, I was in a fabric store one day where I saw a design of violets and I asked the store clerk for a swatch of the fabric for my manifestation book. Years later, when I got to have the Center to live in, Waverly, the maker of the fabric, had sold that particular pattern to Target and everything I could imagine wanting, sheets, curtains, comforter, wallpaper border, pillows, ceramics for the bath, shower curtain, dishes, etc, were all available for me to have. I've never tired of the pattern.

Years ago I met a woman in Ben Lomand, CA, who had a benefactor who provided a place for her to run a retreat center; the person gave her life estate to the property, which meant she could live there as long as she desired or as long as she lived. I wrote that down as one of my desires. Years later I was living in a rental property when the owner decided she wanted to sell the property. I began to look for another place to live. One of the things I had written down was that I desired a view of a large body of water. The first house my soul directed me to look at had a view of the city water tower across the street. I had to laugh and go back and rewrite the desire to view of a river, lake or creek. Soon after, a friend in Denver called and said she had been asked by her soul to refinance her home and to take out her equity to purchase a home for me to live in and to use for the Namaste Enrichment Center, Inc.. It is important to remember other people are also listening to their souls and some are brave enough to follow their soul's suggestions even when it means taking risks. My friend bought the house we now live in and use for the retreat center.

The things the house didn't have that were on my list: a sun room, decks and koi pond were created during the first year. I borrowed money to build the sunroom from friends in Denver and paid on it monthly. Before I called the builders to get a bid on building the sunroom, I asked my soul what it would cost and the reply was, "About $15,000." So when the salesperson came and gave me a bid of $26,900, I told him he was the wrong person to do the job. He asked, "What do you mean?" I explained that God had said the job should cost $15,000. He said, "Just a minute." He began to write again on his clipboard and in a few minutes asked, "Could you live with $15,800?" I agreed it was close and asked him how he could come down so much on his price and he stated, "If God said I should charge around $15,000, I guess I'd better get with the program."

I never liked the color the bank had painted the wooden upper story of the house so when it needed to be repainted a few years later I asked the owner if we could afford to have the upper story covered in vinyl siding. Neither she nor I had the money to accomplish my desire. She attempted to refinance the house to take out money to get the siding, but nothing seemed to work. I placed a picture of what the house would look like with the siding beside my telephone and every time I answered the phone I energized the picture of my desire.

At this time, one of my jobs for the soul was to go to all of the Indian casinos in Oklahoma to set up vortexes of positive energy in each one to bless the people who worked there and the people who came to gamble. Every time I went to a certain casino I would see the same man no matter what day I went or what time of day I went. I never spoke to the man, but watched him intently because he always won. A few days later a crew of men started putting what I considered to be my siding on my next door neighbor's house. I was angry and asked God, "What part of my address did you not get?" After stewing for a while I went over and asked a workman if he would ask his boss to come over to give me a bid on what it would cost for them to put siding on my house. When their boss showed up at my front door it was the man from the casino. You can imagine my surprise. I tried to convince him that if he started the job the money would come. He stated that he believed in God, but that he just wasn't that trusting about money. However, He did agree to do the job the day after I had the money, which was a concession on his part.

Years ago I heard of a conversation Deepak Chopra had with Maharishi, the leader of the TM movement. Maharishi told Deepak that it was his intention to build meditation temples all over the World. This was years before Deepak wrote his books on manifestation. Deepak asked Maharishi, "Where is the money going to come from to do this?" Maharishi replied, "From wherever it is now." I decided to look at my situation from that viewpoint and began to affirm the money is on its way from wherever it is now. A few days later a friend called from Minneapolis and asked, "What's going on with you? Spirit says I'm supposed to be a part of whatever is going on with you." I explained about the siding, the man from the casino and about our being unsuccessful in restructuring the current loan. She indicated that she might be able to lend us the money for the siding. After a few weeks I had not heard back from her and assumed her husband had been unwilling to make the loan. We were all meeting in Sedona for the next Namaste Gathering and she and her husband joined us. She took me to the side and apologized for not calling me back. I told her I understood and not to worry, the money was on its way from wherever it was to where I needed it to be. She said her husband was reluctant to loan the money to Judi since he didn't know Judi, but that he would be willing to buy the house from Judi and restructure the mortgage to pay for the siding as well as paying off the loan for the sunroom. They had also decided to give me life estate to the property and to be responsible for all the maintenance.

When I left Oklahoma City to travel in 1985, my soul asked me to sell all my belongings except what would fit in my car, which I did. They assured me that in the future when I needed furniture, etc., again it would be provided. In 1991, when I moved back to Oklahoma City, the friend who had loaned me her furnished condo in New Mexico offered me the furniture contents of the condo, stating that she had two other homes and didn't want to have a garage sale.

During the years I was traveling, I had very little income. My children came of the age that it was time for them to go to college. I wrote in my manifestation journal, "I now accept being able to offer my children higher education." A few days later a man called from Arizona and said during his meditation that Sprit had suggested that he offer my children higher education, and wanted to know what that would involve. Only one of my children took him up on his offer and gained her degree. Again, I offer the idea to you that other people are listening and are sometimes brave enough to follow their guidance.

A few years ago I wrote that I now accept receiving $30,000 to be able to take off a year to write and finish some of the books I had been working on. I attended a workshop in Minnesota and there was a man there whose family is wealthy and his job is to disburse money from the family foundation. After the conference we were walking down the hall and he said to me, "I think I've made a mistake. I think I've contributed to the wrong Namaste." The next morning at breakfast the director of another Namaste organization tossed a check from his foundation for $30,000 in front of me. My immediate thought was that he had corrected his mistake and that the check was mine. The other person did not know of the error and demanded that I read for her to tell her how her soul wanted her to use the money. You can imagine this was one of the most difficult lessons of my life.

GOD IS THE SOURCE OF MY SUPPLY

There is a continuous movement toward me of the supply of money and all that I need and desire to express my fullest life, happiness and action. I desire, intend, deserve and now gratefully accept I AM a prosperous person whose wallet is always filled with cash and my mailboxes are always filled with negotiable checks made payable to me or to Namaste of Oklahoma. I AM always able and willing to pay all of my financial obligations before they are due. I AM totally debt free through financial abundance.

We can never have enough money to make us feel secure. Money can be stolen, burned, devalued and destroyed. Never make your feelings of security dependent on the amount of money you have. Develop financial serenity and what you have will feel like enough.

I now accept total financial freedom and abundance. My good is assured me by God, the Indwelling Essence of my life.

I AM free to be myself and free to follow Spirit's suggestions. I agree to express that which is ready to express through me now from my soul.

I stand in the midst of eternal opportunity, which is forever presenting me with evidence of its full expression.

I AM peace, joy, happiness and contentment. I AM the spirit of joy within me. I AM the spirit of peace within me, of poise and power.

There is One Life and that One Life is expressing consciously through me now. I now release any blockages or beliefs I have had to allowing total financial abundance, freedom and health to be mine now.

I see my bank account and my wallet continually filled with all sufficiency to meet every need with surplus to share.

I AM totally debt free through financial abundance.

It is important to remember to ask and to ask in writing. We are in the middle of the Fourth dimension. The Laws of the Fourth dimension are different than the Laws of the Third dimension. In the Fourth dimension, in order to allow our souls to assist us, our desires must be in writing.

SOONER OR LATER WE REAP THE FRUITS OF OUR THOUGHTS

We are responsible not only for holding visions of our personal desires, but also for the desires for the Earth and all of Humanity. We came to make a difference. We came to demonstrate the Law of Attraction in a positive manner. We came to co-create our version of Heaven on Earth. Please take the time to think about it and ask your soul to show you your true heart's desires. Give up any, "Yes, but," mentality. If it can work for me, it can work for you.

4.

How to Manifest Miracles in Your Life

Manifestation is the act of making something invisible become visible. It is the act of turning something abstract into something concrete and something potential into something real.

I personally think of it as the art of fashioning a co-creative, synchronistic, mutually supportive relationship between my inner creative energies of my mind and Spirit. I think of it as personally adding something positive to the larger World.

It feels like a metaphysical, mystical, magical way to live my life that makes it possible for me to bring into my life what I need or desire when normal methods either have failed to bring it or I don't seem to be able to create what I desire by purchasing it.

Manifestation seems for me to work in unpredictable, unanticipated magical ways. When I first heard of manifestation I started with attempting to create parking spaces when none seemed to be available. Then I moved from that to manifesting money to pay my bills and the money would come from unexpected places and come exactly when I needed it without excess beyond my need.

Early on, my manifestations seemed to happen coincidentally or synchronistically beyond the power of my efforts. The things that began to happen seemed miraculous.

I learned that deliberate manifestation uses the resources of my mind and Spirit and goes beyond the normal way of getting what I desire. I began to realize that I was manifesting constantly either consciously or unconsciously with my thoughts so I decided to become more deliberate in the way I think.

At first I really "worked" at it and that did not seem to cause what I desired. I finally realized I was trying too hard to "control" how things could or would come to me. I learned to be more relaxed about it after I had written out my desires I left the "how" it was going to happen to God or the Universe. I realized God is infinitely more creative than I can imagine.

I began to realize that there are forces woven into the fabric of my being that are the same as the beingness of everything else in the World as well. Everything in the Universe, including me, is made from the same stuff and that my thoughts and the Law of Attraction was what was bringing me what I desired. I began to believe that manifestation is a spiritual practice not just a mental practice and that when I aligned me, my desire and my motivation with the deepest energies of creation, things happened more quickly and in very unusual ways.

The more I began to be aware of my thoughts and began to think deliberately the fewer times I manifested limitations and frustrations. I became aware of how many doubts, fears, and negative beliefs I had inherited from my parents. So I attempted to reprogram my sub-conscious where these beliefs were stored. I began to rethink what I had been told about myself and began to affirm my worthiness, attractiveness and my intelligence.

I began to realize the creative part of my consciousness works in a more abstract free-flowing way and it does better when I don't attempt to control it. I found it was best to honor and respect these forces and to work with them rather than attempting to control them. I learned to participate rather than to control. I learned that manifestation worked best when I thought of "being" rather than getting or controlling.

My first series of big manifestations came when my soul asked me to quit being a banker and commit to being an artist. My sub-conscious contained a belief that artists are always starving and that I had no artistic talent. I also knew I did not want to be a starving artist. At that time I had $105.00 in the world and all my bills were due. My soul in meditation asked me to create a line of hand painted greeting cards. It was suggested that I purchase parchment paper and watercolors. Since I had so little money, I bought a child's set of school watercolors and I found a source for parchment paper. I was given directions from my soul to tri-fold the paper and I was given sayings in meditation that my soul wanted to use in the cards. I had taken a calligraphy course before I left Texas to move to Oklahoma City. I argued with my soul that I had no talent or education in art, but my argument did not seem to affect what the soul believed. The first time I sat down to attempt to paint, a flower with a butterfly suspended over it came out of the brush. I was fascinated watching myself do something I didn't know how to do. I made as many cards as I had paper for.

After about a week I woke up one morning to rain. I was completely out of cash and only had one credit card left that in an emergency I could charge $285.00. I meditated and the message was to go to go to the neighborhood Albertson's store. I argued, "It's raining outside, I'm not dressed, I haven't showered, my hair's not done and I have no makeup on." The message was repeated over and over. I finally stopped arguing, but didn't get dressed up, I pulled on a sweat suit and went to the Albertsons as I was without makeup; I was disgusted at being expected to go out in the rain to a grocery store when I had no money.

I was new to meditating so following my soul's suggestions often felt confusing to me, and I had no one in my life with whom to discuss what was happening to me. I walked through the grocery store with an empty grocery cart wondering how weird things were going to get, wondering if the peas were going to light up and begin to talk to me. After a short time I heard a man's voice say, "What are you doing? I haven't seen you in the longest time." I turned and looked toward the voice and saw the Rainbow Bread man putting bread on the rack. He had often come to my window at the bank to get his check cashed every Friday. How he recognized me out of the bank and in my sweats was a miracle. I replied, "I'm not at the bank anymore."

"I know that when I go there you haven't been there. What are you doing now?" I hesitated to tell the Rainbow Bread man that God had designed a line of greeting cards and was looking for a place to market them.

"I'm painting greeting cards," I said.

"Where do you market them?" he asked.

"I don't know anything about marketing," I admitted.

"You should market them here. There are eight stores in the Oklahoma City metro area and they are open twenty-four hours a day. All the people in charge of marketing in that department are going to be here tomorrow from Tulsa and I can get you an appointment with them and you can show them what you have."

I didn't know what to say. I was flabbergasted. I finally said, "OK."

"Give me your phone number and I'll call you tomorrow with the time and location for you to meet the district manager."

He didn't even write the number down, but assured me he would remember it. He did call and I took a basket with some sample cards to the store he indicated. All the time I was thinking, "This is ridiculous marketing a handmade product made by one woman in a national chain store is not good business. Surely this guy is going to laugh in my face."

I was led to the back of the store and met the district manager. He very patiently looked at each card and read each one of them. When he looked up he said, "These are lovely and amazing; we definitely want to carry them, but you will need to furnish the racks as we can't put them on the racks with the national brand cards. You'll need to get eight racks and bring them back to the back door of each store, with enough cards to fill them. I'll notify the stores that you are a new vendor. Can you begin bringing them in on Monday?"

I nodded and thanked him still not believing that he had accepted them. I had no idea where to get racks or how I would pay for them. I returned home and meditated again. I received an impression of the Yellow Pages. When I looked under greeting cards I found the name of a wholesale greeting card company.   I called the number and a man answered. I asked if he had any racks that didn't have a company name on them that would fit the dimension of my cards. He began to laugh. I asked why he was laughing. "Lady, I've got them hanging from the rafters. Someone ordered them in 1977 and went out of business before they ever picked them up so I got stuck with them. I can sell them to you for 1977 prices. How many do you need?"

"I will need eight," I replied. "How much will they cost?"

"I can let you have them for $100 a piece."

"When can I pick them up?" I asked.

"I'm going out of town in a little while, but I'll be back and you can pick them up Sunday afternoon if you meet me at my warehouse at one o'clock."

I agreed and hung up the phone and went back into meditation to ask God how I was going to pay for the racks. "Write a check. I'll get you the money before the check gets to the bank on Monday."

Once again I was flabbergasted and unbelieving that this was what God really expected of me. I knew if I wrote a hot check for $800 and God didn't cover it that I could never be bonded to be a banker again (the only thing I was trained to do) and that anything over $700 was considered a felony and I could go to prison.

"And I would like you to attend a seminar this weekend called The Silva Method of Healing," the words in the meditation continued. I called the people who taught Silva and asked if the seminar was full and how much it cost. Of course it cost $285, what was left on my only remaining credit card.

I registered and showed up on Saturday morning.

During the first lecture I was distracted by seeing a good looking, older white-haired gentleman standing in the doorway to the meeting room. He looked familiar to me. At the break I went over to him thinking that if I looked at his name tag that I would remember from where I knew him. Standing in front of him and reading his name tag I realized that I didn't know him and was then embarrassed that he would think I was trying to pick him up with the oldest line in the world, "Don't I know you from somewhere?" I excused myself mumbling, "Must have been in another lifetime." I didn't even believe in past lives at this point, but I just wanted to get away. I returned to my seat and bowed my head still embarrassed. He soon came over to where I was sitting and asked if he could take me to lunch and that maybe in talking we could figure out where we knew each other from. I didn't have enough money left to buy my lunch so it seemed like a good idea that he take me to lunch. I showed him the greeting card samples at lunch and told him about the message I received. He was impressed and admitted that he was now retired and attempting to do what was happening to me. He asked if he could take me to lunch again the next day, but I told him I needed to pick up racks for my greeting cards and would be late getting back to the seminar. He said he would save me a seat and made me promise to come and sit with him when I returned and I agreed.

Writing the hot check was one of the most difficult things I've ever done. I was so tense when I returned to the seminar that I could not talk. The speaker had already begun so I quickly took my seat beside the man who was expecting me to sit with him. He smiled as I took my seat and soon placed his hand on my leg under the table and leaned over and in a very loud whisper asked, "Did you get your racks?" He was wearing hearing aids so I soon realized he had no idea how loud he was "whispering." I was so scared I was mute. He said it again even louder, "Did you get your racks?" I had not told him that I did not have the money and that I was going to pay for them with a hot check. I turned to him and nodded to indicate that I had purchased the racks. He then said in his loud whisper, "How much did they cost?" I thought "that is my business, that is God's business, I don't know you and get your hand off my leg," but again I was too scared to even talk. Again he repeated his loudly whispered question, "How much did they cost?" I wrote $800.00 on a piece of paper and shoved it over to him to try to get him to shut up. In a few minutes he took my hand under the table and put paper in my hand. I felt relieved that we were going to write notes instead of loudly whispering and letting everyone in the room know that I had committed a felony.

When the speaker quit I took my hand out from under the table and opened it. He had filled my hand with hundred dollar bills. I pointed at the money and stammered, "What is this?"

He replied, "Its money."

"Well I see that, but why are you putting it in my hand? I can't borrow it from you. I have no collateral and I don't know if I will ever make enough money to give it back to you."

"Who asked you to give it back? You don't understand; before I left Texas to come up here for this seminar my soul asked me to go to my safety deposit box and take out eight $100 bills and bring them with me. I never carry cash with me when I travel; I always use credit cards. I realized this morning when I woke up that Spirit has been showing me an image of you in my dreams for weeks and that is why I thought I recognized you. I never watch TV other than for the news, but a week before I came to Oklahoma City I sat in the middle of the floor for four nights and watched a movie called *The Thornbirds* and cried with frustration for the priest in the movie who was in love with a woman he could not have. When you told me the story about your priest friend yesterday at lunch, I realized that he was contacting me through the movie to lead me here to help you."

I began to cry. He put his arms around me and assured me that he was gladly giving me the money to help me to get the business started that God wanted to create through me and that he couldn't do what I was doing, but that he was sure he was to help. He took my phone number and left to return to Texas to his wife.

I covered the check, put the racks and cards in each store on Monday and was appalled to find out that I would not be given a check for six weeks because it would take that long for them to set me up as a new vendor through their home office in Salt Lake City. I had to begin to borrow 10, 20 and 30 dollars from people I hardly knew to buy the paper and envelopes to continue. I had to paint twenty hours a day to keep up with the sales. I was suffering from sleep deprivation and fear when one morning the phone rang and woke me.

Groggily I said, "Hello."

"How are you doing?" my benefactor's cheerful voice inquired.

"Not well. I've created a monster and I can't paint fast enough to feed it," I blurted.

I explained to him that they had not paid me for the cards and wouldn't be paying me for at least six weeks when I would be set up on their computers as a new vendor and that I was of necessity borrowing money to buy the paper and envelopes from people I hardly knew.

"Haven't you gotten your photocopy machine yet?" he asked.

I completely lost it and started yelling at him, "You stupid son of a bitch you've obviously never been broke in your life. I'm borrowing money for paper, I'm behind on all my bills and have no money for food or gas and you think I can buy a photocopy machine that costs several thousand dollars?" Sleep deprivation and fear had made me crazy.

"Calm down, calm down, I'm coming to Oklahoma City tomorrow to see a doctor there and I'm supposed to buy you a photocopy machine so you can do the calligraphy on a white sheet of paper and then photocopy the words onto the parchment paper and you can paint twice as many cards and they will still look hand printed."

My Mother had always warned me to never take money from men, because they would then expect to have sex with me. I was taken aback by his offer and thought, "Maybe I can get the price of my body up so I can comfortably negotiate it later or this man really is being sent by God and I'm too tired and sacred now to argue."

"What time will you arrive?" I asked.

"I'll leave early and get there in time to take you for lunch. Why don't you go down today and find the right machine and then we can just go purchase it after lunch and get you started using it," he suggested.

"OK. I'll see you around noon." I sat back against the head of the bed stunned and confused wondering if Edward was influencing this man or was God. I was too tired to care.

That afternoon I dressed and went downtown to a business machine store and watched a demonstration of various copy machines and chose the one the salesman thought would work best for what I needed. Bill, the man from the seminar, arrived about noon and we went to lunch and then purchased the machine. We brought it to my apartment in the trunk of his car and we were standing before it reading the manual and figuring out how to use it when he asked me about my financial situation.

"My credit cards are all maxed out, my bills and rent are all passed due and I have no money for food, gas or paper and envelopes," I confessed.

"Give me your credit cards," he more or less demanded. I knew I could not legally continue to use them and figured he was going to take them to keep me from trying to and getting into trouble so I gave them to him. He left and I thought he went on to the doctor and left for his return to Texas, but about two hours later I heard a knock on the door and there he was. He handed me the cards and receipts where he had gone to the bank and paid off $4,000.00 in credit cards so I could continue to fulfill my obligations to Albertson's and pay my bills. Once again I began to cry from exhaustion and relief. He also handed me a miniature cassette tape recorder and explained that Spirit had indicated that he should stop at the Radio Shack and buy the tape recorder for me, because I was going to write some books and that I would speak the information into the tape recorder and that someone else would type them up for me. I had been given the request in meditation that I would be expected to write books in the future, but felt as limited about writing books as I had about painting and marketing. I had been assured by Spirit that, "Bach will help you." I had no idea what that meant other than the book I had purchased to read to Edward in the moving van when I left Texas was called *Illusions* and was written by Richard Bach and I certainly had no idea how I would ever meet him.

I gratefully accepted the recorder and credit cards and his help. He then asked," What are we supposed to do now?"

"While you were gone I meditated and Spirit suggested that I go to Hurst, Texas to do a healing on a woman's heart there. I met a woman in the lobby at the Silva seminar who has a daughter who lives in Hurst who is facing heart surgery. The woman asked me what I do and I showed her the greeting cards and she said her daughter has started a greeting card company and the cards are almost identical to the ones I've created. Her daughter's company is called dr originals, all lower case letters and the paper and envelopes and messages are almost identical to the ones I created only she is a pen and ink artist, which made her cards easier to reproduce. I was told to name my company bj originals all lower case letters.

He suggested I call the mother of the woman in Hurst and ask her if her daughter would be receptive to having me visit. I did and she indicated she had spoken with her daughter and that she would love to meet me. Bill said he was on his way to Dallas to visit his cousin and that I could ride with him and that he would buy me a one way ticket to return to Oklahoma after I had met with her. On the way to Dallas I read him some of the cosmic information I had received in meditation. When we were approaching Dallas he asked if I would be willing to go to dinner with him and his cousin and that he thought it would be a good idea for me to meet his cousin because he had been a member of the national board of the Church of Religious Science and had taken Silva. He was a meditator and a professional artist. I agreed and we went to dinner. His cousin was an interesting man and asked me lots of questions about how I had begun to meditate and receive messages. He admitted he had not been meditating recently, but that after meeting me he would once again begin to meditate. At the end of the evening he said, "I have a cousin I think would really like to meet you."

"Where does your cousin live," I asked.

"He lives in California," he replied.

"Well, I'm never going to California. My car wouldn't even make it to Dallas so I had to ride with Bill. My car currently uses more oil than it does gas."

"What is your cousin's name?" I asked.

"His name is Marcus Bach," he answered.

"Really, do you think he has any connection to Richard Bach," I asked.

"Marcus is Richard's uncle," he said.

"What does Marcus do for a living?" I asked

"He writes metaphysical books for Unity Church," he answered.

"In that case you had better give me the information; maybe I can communicate with him by mail."

He wrote out the information and Bill took me to Diana Roger's apartment.

When he dropped me off he said it would be the last time we would see each other or be in communication, since he knew his personality well enough to know that if we continued to see each other that he would begin to expect us to have a sexual relationship, and that he knew that was not what our relationship was to be about. He kissed me on the cheek and drove away and never contacted me again.

Diana and I fell into easy conversation. She suggested I go to bed early and the next day I did the energy transfer into her heart. I had panicked my way through the seminar dealing with Bill and buying the racks and writing the hot check, so I remembered very little of what the speaker had said about doing healing, but Diana reminded me that my job was to transfer the energy and that her job was to use it.

I flew back to Oklahoma City the next day. That next weekend I attended the local Science of Mind church that Bill's cousin had recommended. He had said it was a place I could meet other people who meditated. I was standing in the church gift shop looking at the book rack when a man I had met at the Silva class spoke to me. He asked, "Have you read this book?" He showed me a copy he had just purchased of a book called *The World of Serendipity* written by Marcus Bach. I started to laugh and explained that I had just met Marcs' cousin in Dallas.

"I don't have time to read the book right now; why don't you take it and read it and return it to me when you come to meditation next week," he suggested.

I gratefully took the book and read it that afternoon. Then I painted and wrote several cards and mailed them to Marcus. The cards were taken from a saying he had used in his book. "Thanks to chance you came my way. Three cheers for serendipity." Years later when I finally did go to California and met Marcus and his lovely wife he still had the cards in his filing system. He was not willing, however, to help me with writing or to introduce me to his nephew Richard. Maybe Spirit meant the music of Bach the composer, or maybe Marcus didn't understand the significance of Spirit's message, or maybe I will still meet Richard, or since Marcus is now in the world of Spirit maybe he will help me from there.

I married the man from the meditation group. My son came to live with me for that nine months and attended school. Since my husband had a son approximately the same age and he daily made breakfast for the boys and took them to and from school, I was free to meditate and paint. After nine months my husband asked me for a divorce. He found he could not comfortably live with someone who was psychic even though when I met him he claimed to be psychic himself.

I was asked by Spirit to sell the greeting card company that I had been running for three years. The afternoon of the day I received the message in mediation to sell the greeting card company. A woman called on the phone and asked if I had ever considered selling the card company and that she and her partner were interested in purchasing it. They came by that afternoon with the check and purchased it. I was then asked to give up the house I had been renting, put my belongings in storage and let my son return to his father for the summer. It was suggested that I keep only what would fit in the car. I was asked by my soul to begin to travel and was told that every day in meditation I would be given the name of the town to drive to and the names of the people I was suppose to find to deliver messages to from the person's soul.

In 1994 the Master Jesus materialized in my bedroom one morning and asked me to start a non-profit organization called Namaste. I had no idea how to start a non-profit organization, but agreed to do it. He intimated that He and I would hold an umbrella of energy under which twelve Namaste retreat centers would be formed. I was stunned and again felt inadequate.

I was intimidated and once again depressed, but followed the suggestions. I soon found that calling strangers and saying that God had given me their name in mediation and could I come by to deliver a message from their soul was the worst cold call anyone would ever be asked to make. The people would either hang up on me, or want to meet me at the Denny's to see what kind of a kook I was, or some would gratefully say, "I asked for a channel two weeks ago, what took you so long to get here?" Those people would take me home with them and take care of me and feed me and let me sleep on their couch for a few days and sometimes even introduce me to other people I had on my list of people to find. I traveled for three months believing that I would return to Oklahoma City after the summer and rent another home and that the children would come back to live with me. Instead the soul asked me to allow the children to remain in Texas, for me to return to Oklahoma City, sell all my belongings from storage and to continue to travel.

I did what was suggested. It was difficult to watch people carry my belongings away from the garage sale, but I did it. Freed from the responsibility of a home and belongings, I continued to travel for 6 years as a homeless person driving from one state to another building my faith muscles and meeting interesting people. I met a woman in Denver named Judi who was asked by her soul to refinance her home in Denver and purchase a place in Oklahoma City for me to have a Namaste retreat center, Judi followed her guidance and I moved into the center in 2002.

When Judi got ready to move from Denver to Oklahoma City, she asked me to be on the lookout for a one story home for sale in Oklahoma City near the Namaste Center. One morning as I was leaving home, I saw a new for sale sign on a one story home. I called Judi about it and she looked on the Multi List and asked me to get the realtor to show it to me. She and I had written up a manifestation list of the things she wanted in her new home. The realtor showed me the house. When we entered the laundry room I noticed an incredibly narrow shower and thought Judi will not fit in that shower nor would I. When the realtor opened the door to it she explained that it is where you drip dry your clothes. I had asked God to give me a sign to let me know if this was to be Judi's house. Judi is very tall and does drip dry her clothes to keep them from shrinking. It was one thing we had not thought to write in her manifestation journal, but it made me sure it was to be her home.

She already had two mortgages going on her home in Denver and her rental property in Clarendon, Texas, so getting a third mortgage before she sold her house in Denver seemed impossible, but she called her nephew in Florida and asked him if could get it done by his company. The program that would make it possible had just been closed out by his company, but he thought to go online and the offer was still available there so he ran through her request and it was accepted.

The older couple who owned the Oklahoma property rented it back from Judi while their retirement apartment was being completed so it was a win/win arrangement for them and her since she had not yet sold her home in Denver. The timing of all of it worked out and she moved to Oklahoma City.

I'm sharing these stories of manifestation with you to indicate several things: that we won't always understand why we are being asked by our soul to do a thing; that we don't have to believe what we desire is possible; that we don't have to understand; and that our job is to show up and to allow our soul to do these things through us, including manifestation.

It is important that we always follow through with any intuitive information that comes to us. I still argue with my soul when things don't seem to make sense logically, but eventually I give up and follow. I often think of following spirit's guidance as a row of dominoes standing on end that represent events and connections that my soul has arranged, and if I follow to the first place the next domino or person or event somehow leads me to the next connection. I've looked back and recognized how many of these I would have screwed up if I had refused to go to Albertson's in the rain, refused to attend the seminar that maxed out my last credit card, or if I had not trusted my soul and refused to write the insufficient check for the racks.

Each manifestation project we begin adds to our information about ourselves, enhances our awareness and enriches our lives

5.

How to Create Your Version of Heaven on Earth

Above the entrance to all of the ancient wisdom temples were the words:

KNOW THYSELF

Because you are the only one you will never leave nor lose, you are the one you have the most responsibility to get to know most intimately. You are the only answer to the questions of your life. You are the only solution to the problems you have created in your life. It is essential that you like yourself, feel you are worthy of respect, admiration and love. It is vital that you believe yourself deserving of all good things. In order to do these things you may have to let go of who you thought you were and what you have assumed your life was about.

WE DO NOT EXPERIENCE THE WORLD AS IT IS.
WE EXPERIENCE THE WORLD AS WE ARE.

We create our reality by our perceptions based on the thoughts, feelings, beliefs and expectations we have of ourselves, others, the World and God. In the beginning it is important to examine and challenge each belief we hold, each perception we have to see if it is truly ours or is a programmed perception that came from our parents, friends, teachers, church officials or the media. If we keep our current views, beliefs, limitations, fears and misperceptions, which are all fueled by the media, we stop ourselves from becoming all we were created to become. To develop our own truth requires introspection, sorting and beginning to reject what we determine is not true about ourselves, the World, the Universe and God.

In my family we were taught self-love equaled being selfish. We were not taught to love ourselves and certainly not to know ourselves. To know ourselves would have required introspection and it was continually stated, "Too much thinking can make you crazy." I grew up to be a master of patching up whatever didn't look good to the outside world. I was proficient at keeping personal matters out of sight and of causing things to look as if they were always running smoothly. Staying in control became a full time job. I accomplished this at severe expense to my health and my own personal desires and feelings, but to the outside world it always looked good.

When I tried to explain how I was feeling to others they told me, "Get over it. You've got everything. What you have should be enough for anyone. Don't make trouble for yourself by wanting something that doesn't exist. Be happy with what you have." They tried to convince me I did not have a problem so I began to feel I was the problem. I thought, "Something must be wrong with me if I can't be happy with this life." I had become a reflection of what I did and had.

When the seismic shift began to happen cracks began to appear and the truth began to seep through the illusion I had been living as my life. When I began to explore my inner life, which is where the books assured me my truth lay, all I found was a garbage heap in the form of fears, shame, anxieties, angers, grief, sadness and regrets. I was plagued by the fear that I was not enough and a deep sense of lack, although I wasn't clear about what I lacked. When I looked inside I was appalled by the numbers of self-deprecating opinions and insecurities I'd been holding inside and keeping at bay by staying overly busy and pretending my feelings didn't matter, because they were uncomfortable to me and made others angry or uneasy when they were expressed. I learned what might make others angry or not like me and I hid those feelings inside.

When I finally located a person who did not think I was crazy, he said, "Stop making yourself wrong about your thoughts and feelings. Instead, consider that your discontent, worry and fear are really personal truths challenging your current reality. In order to change you must first recognize that you are stuck and agree to do what it takes to become unstuck." The very thought was frightening. I somehow knew that if I changed, I would experience repercussions from all the people around me.

I found that the search to find out who you really are requires a willingness to look closely at what you are not, the false beliefs, the things hidden in the dark place inside you. What is required is that we observe what is there and decide if we want to keep it. Is this the truth and does it serve me now? If it no longer serves you. allow it to float away in a balloon of knowing. Always replace it within yourself with an affirmation that is your new truth, your new perception about yourself, the World, God.

I found that when my mind would fall asleep on the job of being willing to look inwardly, my body could be counted on to wake me up; I could feel the "feather" of my intuition and be brave and follow it, or I could ignore it and wait for the two-by-four experience that would make clear the truth I was ignoring.

Some two-by-four experiences are auto accidents, loss of a job, lack of purpose, depression, loss of a loved one, addictions, rape, a near death experience, insomnia, divorce, bankruptcy, illness, loss of home space, an unplanned pregnancy, personal injury, having your home broken in to, having your car stolen, finding out your spouse or partner has been unfaithful, losing your purse or wallet. Life's two-by-fours are great awakeners, but initially they can be so painful we only want the sleep of depression. We may be too stunned by the pain, fear, resentment, anger or upset to see the value or lesson of the experience. It takes courage and time to go beyond trauma. What is important is waking up to answer the recurring knock of the feather or the two-by-four, because then we can transform our lives and thereby transform the World.

Once I was brave enough to overcome the belief that I should ignore my feelings, I found that what happens inside me is what makes my life work. If I ignore what I'm feeling and thinking my life will not work in my favor.

The greatest obstacle to our attaining anything we desire in life is our "comfort zone". Our comfort zone is our familiar way of functioning automatically or without consciously thinking about what we are doing. The same thoughts, followed by the same actions, reap the same results. To do the same things day after day in our lives and expect a different result is a form of ignorance, ignorance of the Law of Cause and Effect. While living in our comfort zones we often resist change, even positive change, because it is unfamiliar. We spend a lot of time and energy protecting and defending the constricted, stress-ridden reality we call our life, our everyday thinking. This is the energy we could rechannel into creating the life we want.

Change is constant and inevitable. The Universe is not static; it does not remain the same. Our bodies are in a constant state of change. The deep ruts we have created in the ways we think and the habits of our everyday activities need to be looked at. Are the results of these thoughts and these behaviors bringing me the life I want? If not, why not? Complaining gets us more of what we are complaining about. Worry gets us more of what we don't desire, because it gives permission for universal energy to go to literally what we are worrying about rather than to what we desire. It wastes our energy and time. To change our lives we must first agree to think differently and to act differently. We must set new intentions of thought and behavior.

Since change is inevitable, the primary purpose of setting goals and intentions is to allow ourselves, to a greater degree, control over the changes in our lives, change by choice, rather than being served "potluck" as a result of allowing others to make our choices for us.

Early on in my life I was hesitant to set goals for fear I would not be able to accomplish them. I thought, "If I never write them down I will never have to feel like a failure if I don't accomplish them." I later learned that if I don't write down my heart's desires my soul has no permission to assist me to accomplish them, because of the Law of Freewill. I learned our purpose is to be co-creators with our souls, to co-create our individual version of heaven on Earth, and thereby to ultimately recreate heaven on Earth globally. It can only be accomplished one life at a time.

If the word "goals" is a buzzword for you, as it was for me, you may need another word. I now use intention or affirmation. I write the intentions in present tense. I affirm "I AM" as often as possible. "I AM" is a reference to our higher Self our God Self, rather than our ego self. Without roles what remains is the "I AM" part of us. This is the part of us that exists before, after and between births. The ego creates the roles. In order not to be in internal conflict, our goals must be in harmony with our basic values, our souls, and our purpose for coming to Earth for this particular incarnation. The I AM, the spark of divinity inside each of us, wants to show us the truth about ourselves, our talents and the peace and magnificence we are capable of manifesting.

I don't recommend you ask yourself, "What do I want or need?" Take a deep breath into your heart and ask yourself, "What is my true heart's desire?" Close your eyes and let an image or answer come. If nothing seems to occur to you take more breaths into your heart and keep repeating the question with each breath. When the answer finally comes "from your heart" rather than from your mind; tears may accompany it, because our true heart's desires are also our soul's desires. We have usually devalued our true heart's desires by claiming we can't have them, so why try to want what you can't have. We tell ourselves things like; I don't have the money, education, time, or talent. I'm too old, too young, too fat, too ill, too committed to my children, to my job, spouse, or parents, etc. God is infinitely creative. These excuses are illusions we have created for ourselves to stop ourselves from disappointment and possible rejection.

Try this exercise daily until you begin to receive responses from your heart, your soul. Then write your desires in present tense as if you are already experiencing that life.

We need to set intentions in all areas of our lives in order to remain balanced.

Health goals
Personal goals
Family goals
Career/work goals
Financial goals
Spiritual or inner development goals
World goals

Our intentions or goals need to be challenging, but believable in order to not be overwhelming. Make sure one goal or intention does not contradict another.

PEOPLE WHO DO NOT HAVE PERSONAL GOALS ARE DOOMED TO WORK FOR THOSE WHO DO.

It is important to write and read our intentions in present tense, because they describe our desired results, our intended life. If we state them in the present tense we are more likely to work to do the next single thing toward accomplishing them now rather than holding them in future context.

I now accept…
I AM now experiencing…
I AM now enjoying…
I AM now grateful for…

Example: I AM now accepting a life filled with joy, adventure, love, beauty, friends, fun and health, with money and time in excess of my needs and desires.

Read your affirmations daily with enthusiasm and emotion. You are sending these messages into your sub-conscious mind to replace the erroneous messages you've held there with your new truth. You are sending these "purchase orders" into the Universe to be acted out to the highest good of all concerned in alignment with the Divine Plan of the Creator.

You may want to write them on 3x5 cards and carry them with you to read anytime you have to wait or to keep a set in the drawer of your desk at work or write them on your computer. You may choose to make a poster of words and pictures that place these desires into your sub-conscious visually. You can also do this in a notebook form. I do all of the above and it has changed my life. We can argue that all that would take too much time, but I can assure you it is time well spent. Writing it out, in as much detail as possible, gives your soul a blueprint of what you desire. It also gives them permission to help you to achieve it. It keeps you focused on action rather than living your life passively, sitting back waiting for the next two by four.

In my case when I breathed and got in touch with my true heart's desire I had to let go of who I thought I was and what I assumed my life was about. I had to give up the familiar for the unknown. In the beginning my goal setting was vague. At that time I could not even begin to imagine the life I have co-created now. I had to begin with what I could believe. Life is a process. Goal setting is a process and can be an ever-changing process. Sometimes after living with an intention for a while I find it isn't truly what I desire and I change or replace it. Setting intentions gives our lives direction, without which we have a tendency to wander around unfocused or to stay in familiar ruts.

For our lives to become different we have to first be able to imagine or pretend (pre-intend) ourselves in different circumstances performing different roles intentionally from our "I AM", our God Selves, our hearts. It is important to remember we are always playing roles. The trick is to write your own script, choose your own costumes, and choose the other characters with whom you want to share this stage of your life. Allow the "I AM" Self to play the role through you by staying in touch with that I AM part of you, by staying deliberately connected to your soul through your heart.

How To Manifest Miracles In Your Life

If you fill out these pages your life will improve.

MONEY, RESOURCES AND INCOME

I desire, intend, deserve and now gratefully accept:

_____
_____
_____
_____
_____
_____
_____
_____
_____
_____
_____
_____
_____
_____
_____
_____
_____
_____
_____
_____

I now accept this or something better into my life, through the grace of God and to the highest good of all concerned. So be it.

PRIMARY LOVE RELATIONSHIP, MATE

I desire, intend, deserve and now gratefully accept a life mate with these qualities:

_____

_____

_____

_____

_____

_____

_____

_____

_____

_____

_____

_____

_____

_____

_____

_____

_____

_____

_____

_____

_____

_____

_____

_____

I now accept this or something better into my life, through the grace of God and to the highest good of all concerned. So be it.

>I now accept and I draw to me true love...
>I draw to myself my right partner,
>the soul whose love serves my soul's highest potential,
>the soul whom my soul enhances
>to its highest potential.
>I draw this partner to me freely and lovingly
>as I am drawn to this partner.
>I choose and am chosen out of pure love,
>pure respect, and pure liberty.
>I attract one who attracts me equally.
>I seek and am found.
>We are a match made in heaven
>To better this Earth.
>
>*Julia Cameron*

It is important after you make your list of the attributes you wish to attract in a partner that you read your list in terms of yourself to see if you are equal to and as developed as the person you are describing that you wish to attract. If you are not you know what to work on within yourself in order to attract the person you desire.

RELATIONSHIPS

I desire, intend, deserve and now gratefully accept:

_____

_____

_____

_____

_____

_____

_____

_____

_____

_____

_____

_____

_____

_____

_____

_____

_____

_____

I now accept this or something better into my life, through the grace of God and to the highest good of all concerned. So be it.

TRAVEL OR VACATIONS

I desire, intend, deserve and now gratefully accept:

_____
_____
_____
_____
_____
_____
_____
_____
_____
_____
_____
_____
_____
_____
_____
_____
_____
_____
_____
_____
_____
_____
_____

I now accept this or something better into my life, through the grace of God and to the highest good of all concerned. So be it.

SPIRITUAL LIFE, SPIRITUAL GIFTS

I desire, intend, deserve and now gratefully accept:

_____

_____

_____

_____

_____

_____

_____

_____

_____

_____

_____

_____

_____

_____

_____

_____

_____

_____

_____

_____

I now accept this or something better into my life, through the grace of God and to the highest good of all concerned. So be it.

COMMUNICATIONS

I desire, intend, deserve and now gratefully accept:

_____
_____
_____
_____
_____
_____
_____
_____
_____
_____
_____
_____
_____
_____
_____
_____
_____
_____
_____
_____
_____

I now accept this or something better into my life, through the grace of God and to the highest good of all concerned. So be it.

CAREER – LIFE WORK

I desire, intend, deserve and now gratefully accept a career or life work with these features:

_____
_____
_____
_____
_____
_____
_____
_____
_____
_____
_____
_____
_____
_____
_____
_____
_____
_____
_____
_____
_____

I now accept this or something better into my life, through the grace of God and to the highest good of all concerned. So be it.

MY BODY – HEALTH – PHYSICAL APPEARANCE AND CONDITION

I desire, intend, deserve and now gratefully accept:

_____
_____
_____
_____
_____
_____
_____
_____
_____
_____
_____
_____
_____
_____
_____
_____
_____
_____
_____
_____

I now accept this or something better into my life, through the grace of God and to the highest good of all concerned. So be it.

EDUCATION AND KNOWLEDGE

I desire, intend, deserve and now gratefully accept:

_____
_____
_____
_____
_____
_____
_____
_____
_____
_____
_____
_____
_____
_____
_____
_____
_____
_____
_____

I now accept this or something better into my life, through the grace of God and to the highest good of all concerned. So be it.

HOME

I desire, intend, deserve and now gratefully accept a home with these features:

_____

_____

_____

_____

_____

_____

_____

_____

_____

_____

_____

_____

_____

_____

_____

_____

_____

I now accept this or something better into my life, through the grace of God and to the highest good of all concerned. So be it.

AUTOMOBILE OR TRANSPORTATION

I desire, intend, deserve and now gratefully accept:

_____
_____
_____
_____
_____
_____
_____
_____
_____
_____
_____
_____
_____
_____
_____
_____
_____
_____
_____
_____

I now accept this or something better into my life, through the grace of God and to the highest good of all concerned. So be it.

CHILDREN AND/OR FAMILY

I desire, intend, deserve and now gratefully accept:

_____
_____
_____
_____
_____
_____
_____
_____
_____
_____
_____
_____
_____
_____
_____
_____
_____
_____
_____
_____

I now accept this or something better into my life, through the grace of God and to the highest good of all concerned. So be it.

STABILITY

I desire, intend, deserve and now gratefully accept these situations in my life to create a feeling of stability:

_____

_____

_____

_____

_____

_____

_____

_____

_____

_____

_____

_____

_____

_____

_____

_____

_____

_____

_____

_____

I now accept this or something better into my life, through the grace of God and to the highest good of all concerned. So be it.

CREATIVE ABILITIES – TALENTS

I desire, intend, deserve and now gratefully accept these talents and abilities:

_____
_____
_____
_____
_____
_____
_____
_____
_____
_____
_____
_____
_____
_____
_____
_____
_____
_____
_____
_____

I now accept this or something better into my life, through the grace of God and to the highest good of all concerned. So be it.

COMMUNITY – ENVIRONMENT

I desire, intend, deserve and now gratefully accept:

_____
_____
_____
_____
_____
_____
_____
_____
_____
_____
_____
_____
_____
_____
_____
_____
_____
_____
_____

I now accept this or something better into my life, through the grace of God and to the highest good of all concerned. So be it.

OPPORTUNITIES

I desire, intend, deserve and now gratefully accept:

_____

_____

_____

_____

_____

_____

_____

_____

_____

_____

_____

_____

_____

_____

_____

_____

_____

_____

_____

_____

I now accept this or something better into my life, through the grace of God and to the highest good of all concerned. So be it.

HEALING

I desire, intend, deserve and now gratefully accept healing for myself and the Earth:

_____

_____

_____

_____

_____

_____

_____

_____

_____

_____

_____

_____

_____

_____

_____

_____

_____

_____

_____

I now accept this or something better into my life, through the grace of God and to the highest good of all concerned. So be it.

EQUIPMENT AND SUPPLIES

I desire, intend, deserve and now gratefully accept:

_____

_____

_____

_____

_____

_____

_____

_____

_____

_____

_____

_____

_____

_____

_____

_____

_____

_____

_____

I now accept this or something better into my life, through the grace of God and to the highest good of all concerned. So be it.

CLOTHING AND JEWELRY

I desire, intend, deserve and now gratefully accept:

_____
_____
_____
_____
_____
_____
_____
_____
_____
_____
_____
_____
_____
_____
_____
_____
_____
_____
_____

I now accept this or something better into my life, through the grace of God and to the highest good of all concerned. So be it.

6.

Our Emotions and Beliefs Affect Manifestation

The relationship between our inner Worlds of consciousness and outer worlds of "objective reality" is the opposite of what our culture teaches. Our World is a reflection and "effect" of Human thought. Human thought is the "cause." The World is not there to create struggle, victimize us, block spiritual progress, or provide us with excuses for our unhappiness. It is there to provide a stage or medium through which all of the dramas of consciousness, from agony to ecstasy, can be played out and reflected upon. Once one grasps this fundamental inversion, whether it manifests in the form of repressed anger crystallizing as a tumor, as in my breast cancer, or your boss failing to acknowledge your contributions at work, your spouse or partner not appreciating your efforts, the door is open to many paths of growth. Without this realization, the chances of becoming stuck in places we don't want to be are significantly increased. Once we realize what we think is what we get, what we think with intense feeling we get to experience even quicker.

In my case I recently became aware that I do not attract male relationships that are with men who are balanced. I have held very negative opinions and beliefs about the male Human population. When I consciously recognized the belief and the result, I wondered how do I manifest something I don't believe exists or something I've never seen. The soul threw a book off the shelf to get my attention. The book suggested that instead of praying for something that I didn't believe existed, I should pray to be healed of my negative beliefs about men in general. As a result of the prayer my primary care physician, who of course happens to be a male, refused to continue to be my physician unless I agreed to a complete physical. While feeling as if I was being held hostage by a male dominated system (the medical system) I resented it, but agreed to the physical; it was easier than changing doctors. I consider myself to be a healthy person, but I needed prescriptions for estrogen, since I've had my internal female organs removed and I need a script for thyroid meds, because I push way too much energy through my pituitary and pineal glands doing the work I do and this affects my thyroid function. I have to have a medical doctor to get these meds.

During the physical the doctor noticed a lump in my left breast, my female side. He made an appointment for me to have a mammogram, which led to a breast biopsy, which led to an MRI, which led to a male surgeon, which led to surgery. The male surgeon is one of the most "present" medical professionals I've ever met. He truly had my highest good in mind, treated me as if I am intelligent, listened and explained everything in great detail in easy to understand terms. It was obvious <u>he had no ego need to seem superior to me</u>. I was amazed.

The second I heard the diagnosis "it is cancer" I mentally made the agreement with my soul that I would do whatever treatments were necessary without fear, but I would not pay for the treatments myself. After I put my clothes back on, I walked into the lobby of the clinic. A woman walked up to me and asked me if I had time to speak with her for a few minutes. I followed her into her office. She was the financial officer of the clinic. She asked me about my income and my occupation. After I described my circumstances, she said she felt she could intervene to get me set up with Medicaid for at least a year which would pay all the expenses of my treatments, which she did. Making agreements with our soul about our desires is an important part of manifestation.

I immediately kept an appointment I had made previously with friends to meet in Denver to celebrate the New Year and to do some energy work on the Rocky Mountain Fault Line. While I was there a male chiropractor and healer I have not seen in over fifteen years called and offered to help me get to the core belief that created the circumstances for the tumor to live in my body. He had changed completely since the last time I had seen him. His ego had diminished to the point that being in the same room with him was comfortable. He had reached a point of allowing his soul to give him intuitive assistance. He muscle tested me in a very awkward position so that my mental attitude could not mask the results of my body giving him accurate answers. He immediately learned from my body that that the stage had been set for the negative belief and mistrust of males had happened at the age of nine in this body and that at the soul level the events being healed happened during the time of the Knights Templar. After the energetic release work we accomplished I immediately felt lighter, but the tumor was still there.

I returned to Oklahoma City. The surgeon accomplished the surgery and I recovered with no pain. I've had lumpectomies before for fibroid cysts and the after effect pain was excruciating. A friend who is a retired nurse volunteered to stay with me for 48 hours after the surgery, which was a great help.

Two weeks later I had an appointment with a male oncologist. He felt there was a discrepancy between the pathology report on the biopsied material and the material from the actual tumor that was sent for pathology testing. These materials were sent to be retested. The oncologist was sure I needed severe chemotherapy followed by six weeks of radiation. Since I still didn't feel I had signed up for anything beyond surgery and radiation I was amazed when I was taken into the chemotherapy room and could see myself sitting in one of the chairs talking with other patients. Through the years I've been consciously working with the soul, one of the things I've trained myself to do is to project myself into the future to see if I can see myself in the possible situation, such as attending a conference, traveling to another city or country or attending a party. If I can see myself there in the projection I know I will be there and I begin to make plans accordingly.

After the biopsy proved the lump was cancer I agreed to the surgery and radiation, but still felt I would not have to have chemotherapy. The biopsy and surgery had already taken two months. The chemo was to take another six months and the radiation another six weeks. I could not imagine giving over nine months of my life to this experience. I renegotiated with my soul in meditation. I've just heard back from the oncologist that he feels I can do with a lower form of chemotherapy, which would only take six weeks, then radiation for six weeks. Next week I went in for another surgery to have a port installed in my chest through which the chemotherapy will be administered.

When I was diagnosed I was amazed and asked the soul, why do I have this? The response was that at the level of my soul I have agreed to have breast cancer and to use both allopathic and alternative methods to correct this imbalance for myself and for Humanity without fear. The fear of cancer and especially breast cancer is high in Human consciousness at this time. For a person to have the dis-ease and to walk through the procedures without fear and to add this to Human consciousness is important. When one Human does as supposedly impossible thing it enters a matrix into Human consciousness that makes it possible for others to accomplish the same task if they choose. I have to admit, however, even though I didn't feel fear, I did feel inconvenienced. When the recommended procedures were mammogram, sonogram, biopsy, surgery, radiation I was able to feel it was a minor inconvenience. Once the treatment procedures were expanded I began to feel it was a major inconvenience. The doctors were all males.

The Earth's frequency is speeding up and things that used to happen slowly and with little intensity are now hitting us fast and hard. The more condensed the energy around and within the Earth becomes the less time it takes for our negative or positive thoughts to express themselves as our reality. The current rash of natural disasters and Earth changes that we see in the news everyday is proof of that. We won't be able to pull together collectively to live in the Aquarian Age if enough individuals don't decide to start on their own path of personal growth. <u>Personal paths must lead away from fear and isolation toward the chance to bring personal power to bear on the problems that face us all.</u>

Matter is really energy. We may know Einstein's famous formula $E=mc^2$, but we don't really believe that the world works that way. Metaphysics really is putting the idea that everything is energy into everyday use in our lives. Energy has flow, usually cyclical. It wants to move. Example: electricity can't stand still; it exists only as an electrical current. In our energy fields we see this manifested as the eternal cycle of giving and receiving and the internal cycle of growth and manifestations. Energy has polarity: +/-, yin/yang, odd/even. In our energy fields we see this manifested as male and female. An energy field has magnetism – it draws like things to it. Examples: gravity, an electromagnet. This is how we create our own reality. Energy seeks balance. Example: a bolt of lightning will always try to ground itself. We can see this in our own energy fields. This balance will become external if there is no internal balance. For instance, a person who gets their sense of worth from taking care of others will usually end up marrying or attracting people who want or need to be taken care of.

Everything is energy and therefore we are energy. The physical form that we think of as our "body" is really four separate energy fields overlaid on top of each other. These four energy fields are the physical, the emotional, the mental and the spiritual. Each one is centered around a focused energy point called a "chakra." There is a physical chakra, an emotional chakra, a mental chakra, a spiritual chakra. These four energy centers, or points, are sort of central "clearing houses" for energy flowing through the body that they represent. That is to say that if, for instance, there is going to be a blockage of energy flow, or "logjam," through the emotional body, the emotional chakra is probably where it will first become evident. Since the emotional chakra is located just below the navel, this blockage might manifest itself as a physical tightening of the muscles in that area or even a constriction in the digestive flow: i.e. a bout of constipation.

There are seven major chakras, the four "lower" chakras, and the three "higher" chakras: the power center in the throat, the "third eye" in the forehead, and the crown chakra on top of the head. The four lower chakras are related to our physical reality, the upper three are more attached to that part of us that is independent of this present incarnation, the soul.

All energies have a specific frequency or vibration. For example, a specific frequency of light would be a particular color, a specific frequency of sound would be a particular pitch or note. Our energy fields are spectrums, with each chakra being a specific frequency in that spectrum. Our "souls," or "higher selves" – or whatever term you prefer—is that highest and most energetic frequency of that spectrum, and our physical bodies are the lowest, densest, and slowest frequency.

Anything that is energy has a specific rate of vibration; this is called its frequency. Remember energy is in constant motion. If something has a frequency it has a sound and a color. Only very small portions of those frequencies fall into ranges in the two scales that our eyes and ears can pick up. Since our energy fields are a collection of different frequencies, like "white" light, they can also be broken down into these same colors. Red is at the bottom end of the rainbow because it has the lowest frequency (travels at the slowest vibration). So, the color red corresponds to our densest and slowest aspect: the physical.

The chakra for the physical body is at the base of the spine in the groin/tailbone region, and it would be red. The emotional chakra is located right below the navel in front of the sacrum bone of your spine and its color is orange. The mental chakra is in the solar plexus right below the sternum and its color is yellow. The spiritual chakra is in the center of the chest, in our heart space and its color is green. The throat chakra, which is our center of power and communication, is blue. The "third eye" or psychic center in the middle of the brain, which we think of as reflected into the forehead, is indigo. Our connection to our higher self is considered the "crown" chakra and is violet.

The important concept to grasp is that Human beings are not just static lumps of matter. We are made of energy fields that affect, and are affected by, the rest of the World. Our energy fields have several different levels that interact with each other and our surroundings. Our physical bodies, then, are just the hard, innermost kernel of an onion-like energy field that floats in the sea of energy that makes up our reality. Our bodies are energy fields. Matter is energy. We are matter. Energy has a flow, therefore we have a flow. A healthy body is the manifestation of a flowing energy field. A blocked or stagnant energy field will manifest as an injury or disease. An affliction of the physical body is caused by a block in our energy field, held in place by an emotion.

But what about accidents, such as dropping a hammer on your foot, how can that be caused by a blocked energy field? If you hold your arm near the energy field of the television screen, the hairs all stand up. That shows that energy fields affect their environment. We know that energy has this "magnetic" property. So if your field contained the belief (an energy) that you couldn't stand up for what was rightfully yours, held in place by the fear of confronting your boss about a raise? Couldn't that magnetically draw an accident to the part of your body that symbolically represents standing?

If everything is energy, then God or the Universe or whatever your idea of perfection is, is also energy. So, as energy beings, we are all part of that perfection. We are all made of the same energy as the rest of the Universe (God included), so we are all connected.

When I say we are all made of the same energy, I am not implying that we have no differences. For instance, the Atlantic and Pacific Oceans are obviously connected and made up of the exact same substance, water. But they have many different characteristics: direction of currents, frequency of storms, temperature, etc. Because they are different expressions of the same thing, we think of them as separate entities; as energy beings, we are the same way. If we accept this concept of connectedness, it makes it much easier to imagine that changes in our energy fields would lead to changes in the flow of energy that is creating the circumstances in our lives. Raising the water temperature in the Atlantic by even a few degrees would eventually affect the quantity and quality of marine life in the Pacific.

The earlier example about the raise and the hammer, would be ludicrous for a beingthat is part of the perfection of the Creator to not have the strength or the right to stand up for what they deserve. So, we see that a block in energy flow is really an "untruth" that blocks the energy flowing through our energy field. "I'm not good enough, handsome enough, beautiful enough, smart enough," "I can't get what I need," "I'll always be alone," etc.—are really just variations of the central "untruth" that we are not part of the perfection of God energy. We hold these untruths in all four of our bodies, physical, emotional, mental and spiritual, all the time, and the manifestation of these blocks into our World causes us much pain and suffering.

Whatever we are holding in our energy fields, truths or untruths, flow or stagnation, is what we create (manifest) in our lives. Our energy fields are the pattern or blueprint of what actually percolates down into the densest and lowest energy level or vibration, the physical reality that we all know.

If a person is holding an untruth in their field (held in place by fear) that says "When things are going good for me, something bad always happens." Say, this person just got a raise at work. Guess what? They try to make a left hand turn through traffic, and the person going the other way just happens to be holding an untruth in their energy field (held in place by guilt) that says "I'm not a trustworthy person." Sure enough, this person is driving a car they borrowed from their mother. If an accident happens; is it Fate, predestination, Will of God, random coincidence, or two corresponding energy fields working together to draw in a situation that will play out both of those beliefs? If we believe that the very fabric of the Universe is energy first and matter second, a situation being drawn together and created by energy is not hard to imagine. <u>Energy is where everything starts and matter is the result</u>. Neither of the people in the accident consciously chose to get in an accident, therefore they can easily take the role of victim rather than to own up to their position as creators of their own reality.

Our untruths can be very deeply buried in our unconscious, yet they are still in our energy field, and they are forming the blueprint from which we create our reality. It is much simpler to chalk it up to "bad luck" and take the other guy to court. Taking that position, however, means that those unconsciously held (and untrue) beliefs will continue to play out in our lives.

Using the analogy of a river, the general shape and course of the river stays petty constant as you look at it from minute to minute (although it changes in the long run), but the water running past you at any given minute is not the same water that was there the minute before. That particular water is quite a ways downstream. Our energy fields are the same way. When everything is going as it should, we are merely the completion of a circuit that connects us to our Higher Self or the Universe. So it is the pattern that the energy flows through, and not the actual energy, that forms what we see.

These "patterns" that channel the energy are our beliefs about who we are and how the world works. Although at some level we hold them to be gospel, these beliefs may, as we have seen, bear little resemblance to the real Truth: we are all part of the same energy as God, the Creator or Perfection. We, like the river, must have flow. If part of the river's current gets diverted from its Perfection (onward flow), that water will form a stagnant pool or eddy. Mosquitoes begin to breed there. Sticks, garbage, and other debris begin to build up, and soon a logjam or block is formed. We are the same way. If we are holding a pattern that deviates from our truth of Perfection, then we get blocked, and stagnant places in our energy field will soon begin to manifest as a physical disease, accident or a diseased life situation pattern, such as attracting relationships with people who are afraid of commitment.

A flowing energy field is a healthy energy field. Our energy fields are sometimes cluttered with other things: mental chatter, stray emotions that aren't stuck (we just forgot to let go of them), even unacknowledged physical needs. It helps to get this energetic "clutter" out of the way before trying to deal with our deep-seated programming or blocks. Meditation is a great tool for clearing ourselves. Regardless of the form your meditation takes, it can help you to release the "static," the random energy that is cluttering up your energy field.

Breathing in and out is a flow of energy. The breath is a very effective way to physically do something to move energy. Thoughts are also energy. Using our Imagination we can add energy to the nerve pathways that will soon carry out any action we have planned. Breath and imagination are two of the most powerful tools for clearing our energy field. You may want to read this portion of the exercise into a tape recorder to use for yourself.

After you have entered meditation through your own method of intention and breath, begin to breathe deliberately into the chakra at the base of your tailbone. Let the breath expand it like blowing on the embers of a fire. See its red color grow brighter and brighter. Don't force it, let the breath activate and begin to feel the energy resonate throughout your physical body. Let physical tensions flow out with your outgoing breath. Feel your shoulders and other chronic tension areas relax. Let your physical body begin to speak to you. It might say something like, "I'm hungry, this seat cushion feels lumpy or it's really warm in this room." Acknowledge each of these messages and then let them go. Breathe them out.

When the physical chakra feels fully activated and each of its voices has been heard and allowed to release, let the breath draw the energy up to your second chakra, the emotional. See it as a ball of energy located just below your navel. Breathe into this point of light which is the center of your emotional body and let it expand, its orange color getting brighter and brighter. Let any emotional voices that need to speak, be heard. "I'm still mad at my sister-in-law for that cheap birthday gift." "I'm worried about all the bills this month." Don't try to fix them, just acknowledge that they are there and let them go. See them float up and out with your breath into your soul, into your I AM Presence. If one emotion screams for attention, reassure it that you will come back to it later and let it float on out so that your emotional space can be clear.

When the emotional chakra feels fully activated and each of its voices has been heard and allowed to release, let the breath draw the energy up to your third chakra, the mental. See it as a glowing point of energy in your solar plexus, just below your "wishbone." As you visualize the yellow color of this chakra, feel the energy field of the surrounding mental body begin to quiet down. Let each of the stray thoughts that come up flow across your internal screen and off the other side. Acknowledge them, but don't let them draw you into conversation. "I wonder if I cleaned out my In-box at work?" "What are we having for dinner?" Breathe them up and out into your soul, your I AM Presence, clearing the space within the body.

When each of the three lower bodies has been cleared and activated, turn your attention to the Heart chakra, the center point of your spiritual body. Imagine it in the center of your chest as a green spark of energy. Breathe into it and see how the breath connects it to the lower three chakras like pearls on a string. As the spiritual body is cleared and activated like the lower three, with each of its voices being acknowledged and released, let the breath strengthen the ribbon of energy that connects them all. Feel it grow into a pole of light that runs all the way through the center of your body. Let any cares or sorrows that are weighing heavily on your heart be whisked up and out with your breath.

Complete the process by extending this shaft of energy up through your neck and out through the top of your head, clearing and activating the three upper chakras along the way: the sky blue throat chakra in your neck; the indigo colored psychic chakra, or the "third eye" in your forehead; and the violet colored crown chakra at the top of your head. See once again how they are all connected like pearls on a string by the stream of energy that now runs all the way through you. Feel how this beam of light connects you through your feet to the central core energy of the Earth and through the crown of your head to your soul, your I AM Presence.

Your energy field is now clean and flowing, visualize an egg-shaped envelope of pure white light that surrounds you and prevents outside energies from flowing into the internal spaces you have created. Meditating and clearing your chakras first can prepare a "blank slate" as you prepare to tackle those deep seated patterns that are blocking your growth.

We each create our individual reality, collectively we create our society. We each contain both male and female energies. Sadly, our male and female parts often do not work together, and are, in fact, openly antagonistic at times. We've gone through history with matriarchy and patriarchy. It is time for an age of balance, what spirit calls androgenarchy. Everything that is happening in our society today, everything that's manifesting, is a direct result of what is happening internally with people.

Child abuse is suddenly exposed publically. Child abuse is not a new thing, but enough individuals have done their internal work to break the cycle. Their parents had an internal imbalance of discipline (masculine energy) and nurturing (feminine energy). They expressed it externally by hurting their kids, but the kids refuse to pass it on.

When we become aware of a block energetically, or an untruth held in consciousness, we can reprogram it. Everything we need and desire is actually energy. "I need money right now," actually means "I need the energy of abundance that money represents for me." All these "things" that we think we need in order to be fulfilled and happy, can really all be boiled down to a specific energy or energies.

We are, as energy beings, made in the image and likeness of God, which means we are the same energy as the Creator and Creation. Therefore, all the various energies found in God can be found within ourselves. We have all those energies within us, but we have to learn how to access them and use them so we can begin to manifest all the "things" we need or desire.

First look at your life and determine if you have a need that is going unmet. Agree to uncover within yourself the untruth that keeps what you desire from being your reality. In the growth cycle, our emotions serve as our teachers. If you have a need that is not being met, you will have an emotion. Emotional pain and distress are little red flags that say "Warning: you have a need that is not being met."

If I remain conscious:
An event happens.
I have an emotional response.
I ask, "What is my need here?"
I become aware an energy, from my heart (my soul),
that would meet my need is now available to me.

With this realization I have grown.
I now have a new quality available in my heart.
I can plan a course of action to express this soul quality.
That action will be supported by a positive feeling
I will now manifest new events in my life.

For example, if someone capitalizes on my idea at work and receives praise from the boss that I feel should rightfully have been mine, I may feel anger. The anger tells me that I have a need going unmet. That is all. Not that I should retaliate in any way, just that I have a need that is going unmet. I was not receiving the energy that I needed from that interaction. Maybe the energy was honor. If the emotion I felt in the same situation was fear. I might be afraid that my co-worker would appear smarter and more efficient to my boss and that I would soon be out of a job. An energy, other than honor, is missing. It is important to determine, what are you not getting? Suppose the co-worker is a friend and the emotion you felt was betrayal. Any of these feelings lets you know you are not holding in your energy field, the energy necessary to magnetically draw in what you want or desire.

If our needs are not being met, we will experience pain. Emotional pain at first (fear, guilt, anger and grief are a few), but if we push the feeling away and do not let it express on the emotional level it will eventually become a physical pain.

Our job then, is to listen to our emotional pain and see where it takes us. The biggest obstacle to this is, owning our emotions. We must constantly remind ourselves that "this emotion is for me and about me." If we fall into the victim of believing that "you made me angry" (or sad, or upset, etc.) or "you caused my pain," then all growth is lost. We will never get to the bottom of our feeling because we just gave it away. If you caused me to be angry, then it is not my anger, it is yours.

If you yell at me, I can feel any one of a number of things, ranging from annoyance that you interrupted my chain of thought, to elation that you finally got that off your chest and now the air is clear. If I end up feeling angry about the yelling, it is because I chose that feeling from a wide range of possibilities. That is the key, if I chose the feeling there is a reason. Staying with our emotions about a particular situation long enough to own them and following them to the "Why" is the first step in the personal growth cycle. The door to awareness is through emotion.

Behind every feeling is a piece of you saying "I want to express." Not,

"I want to tell them off, but "I want to express me for me." Life really is all about you.

Many feelings are uncomfortable enough that we want to make the pain go away as quickly as possible. So we take a little taste of them and then quickly shove them back down, or onto someone else. This doesn't move them out of the way, and we don't get the issue (the "Why") that is behind the feeling. However, if we can stay with the emotions long enough – not judging it, not pushing it away, just sitting right in the middle of it – then it begins to detach itself from the situation or other person and begins to reveal something about us. Instead of "you made me angry by yelling at me," it becomes "when you yelled, I became angry because _____."

That empty blank is our "Why" and we may have to repeat that statement over and over to ourselves, letting the blank space just hang there, but eventually something will come up to fill it. When it does, we have our answer. "When you yelled, I became angry because...I was scared and my anger feels protective to me."

There may be several layers to our answer, but we keep asking "why" until we get to the rock bottom. You'll know you've reached the bottom when all you have left is a statement about who you are. Why did I get scared when you yelled? Because "I don't feel safe when other people express themselves with intensity." There! Rock bottom. A statement about who I am. I am a person who lacks the energy of safety in this situation. If you have uncovered the issue behind your emotion, there will always be an energy missing. Remember, that is what the emotion is all about – a need going unmet – and needs are energies, not "things."

Once you have stayed with the emotion long enough to detach it from the circumstances and get to the "Why," the second step is to replace the untruth ("I lack safety") with your truth (I am made of the same energy as God, Perfection, my I AM Presence. I most certainly do have the energy of safety in me, and I can bring it to bear in any situation I choose.").

The physical is the actual event, the yelling. The emotional is being aware of the feelings. The mental is holding focus for long enough to get to the rock bottom belief. So that leaves the spiritual body. Our spirit is the sum total of all the qualities that make us up: our compassion, our love, our sense of adventure and play, our capacity for sharing, to name a few. So when I say "I am made of the same energy as God and I do have the energy of safety in me somewhere" – that somewhere is our spiritual body, centered in our heart chakra. We are made of the same energy as God. Our spiritual bodies contain all the same energies, qualities as God. The problem is that we have not claimed very many of those energies as our own. We generally are hanging on to a multitude of untruths that assert such things as "I am not enough," "I cannot have safety," or "I don't deserve."

The first step in the growth cycle is an awareness of your need. The second step is claiming your truth. Tune in to your spiritual body the same way you did to your emotional body. Breathe into your heart, your spiritual chakra. Speak into that spiritual space, "I need safety." You will feel an energy response. The energy of safety will begin to be sent to you from your soul. Claim the energy. "I AM part of the energy of God and I do have the energy of safety in me and I can call it forth whenever I choose." If you have never had safety in your life before, the energy may feel unfamiliar and elusive. Part of the process then, is sitting in the middle of that energy, just like you did the emotion, until you know the feel of it inside and out. When we claim a new part of ourselves in this way, we have expanded our energy field. This is true growth.

Try going back through your day (or week) and bring to mind situations in which you were aware of a strong emotional response. Then go through the growth cycle process with each one. Follow the process through your four bodies. Physical: an event happens. Be aware: Is this really about me? What are my reactions?

Then there is the emotional: How do I feel about this? "I choose to feel this way because_____?" Our job is to stay focused through all the layers of "Why" until we get to the need at the rock bottom... the statement of who we are around the event.

Then there is the spiritual: what energy or quality could I incorporate into my field that would meet this need?

If you visualize this progression as a flow chart through your four bodies and their corresponding chakras, you will notice that the flow of this cycle is upward. The growth cycle is about following the energy of a situation up from the lowest and densest vibration of our spectrum to the highest and most energetic.

You will probably also notice that the Male aspects of our energy field, the physical and mental, play a rather passive role in the growth cycle – awareness and focus. Our female side provides the activity during this part of the cycle – the discovery of our need (emotional) and the claiming of our truth (spiritual). If our male and female aspects are out of balance, we can get stuck at some point in the process and just keep repeating one segment instead of growing beyond it. For example: If a person is most comfortable in their mental body and allows that body to be overactive;

it will try to and take charge and the male energy will be out of balance. They may not be able to maintain a focus long enough to get through all the layers of emotion and find the real need. If that is the case, the cycle stops right there and the same issue keeps coming up in that person's life. They continue to have the same emotional reactions and get discouraged that they can't seem to break out of this pattern.

If your physical response is to "do something" or "fix the situation" before you can even be with the emotion and get to the need, then the physical body is too active and is probably getting in the way of your awareness. Calm down the physical body. Go back to the beginning of the process and make an effort to remain aware. Focus on each body individually, step by step. Is each body doing its job?

Growth is endless. We learn a small piece of who we are, manifest that piece, and that will lead us to a new lesson or another aspect of the same lesson that we didn't get the first time. Remember life is a game. Learn to play without taking every event personally, other than how does it provide an opportunity for me to grow, for me to learn more about myself?

If we make a prayer, which is expressed on a higher frequency, it can make a change on one end of the spectrum, eventually percolating down into a lower vibration (the physical or mental body) as a large or perceptible change.

Am I healed of my negative beliefs about the males of our species and my own maleness? No, but I'm making progress. The more I agree to be healed, both in my own maleness and in my attitudes, the more possible it has become for me to be physically and emotionally healed and for me to bring males into my life that are conscious, ego diminished and helpful. When I heal my beliefs, I can heal my body.

Whatever it is you desire you must become this in your mind, words, feelings, desires, and actions. Act as if, and you are. The outer must correspond to the inner.

7.

Living Our Best Life

Our lives are not so much controlled by the size of our brains as they are by the size of our thinking. There is magic in thinking big. Our environment will attempt to tell us there is too much competition for the top spots in life. This is not true. We have the life we have as a direct result of what we think and even more so as a result of what we believe we deserve and what we believe is possible. "Fate" only affects us if we don't bother to control our own thinking.

> "AS ONE THINKETH IN HIS HEART, SO IS HE."
> — The Bible

> "Great men are those who see that thoughts rule the World."
> — Emerson

> "There is nothing either good or bad except that thinking makes it so."
> —Shakespeare

> "Life is too short to be little."
> — Disraeli

> "We don't get what we deserve; we get what we believe."
> — Wonder Woman

To live our best lives we must first understand ourselves. We can only understand ourselves by listening to what we are thinking. We must understand and admit what we love and what we love to do. If we agree to work at jobs we hate, if we agree to stay in relationships that are not satisfying, if we feel unworthy, we will not be living our best lives. Watching what we are thinking is the beginning of wisdom. To "Know Thyself" is the goal. How can we know ourselves if we are unwilling, or afraid, to listen to ourselves? No one else can tell us what we believe or what we think. Self-knowledge is the key to living our best lives. Our souls love to think big.

Before we can be successful, we must believe we can be. We must believe we deserve success, happiness, prosperity and health. I was only able to do this when I finally found the true definition of myself and learned to believe it. I AM God operating through the personality of bj King for the benefit of Earth, all life on the Earth and beyond. This is the truth of who I AM. If you insert your name this is also the true definition of you.

The soul created our bodies. Our bodies were created to be vehicles through which our soul would have a vehicle, brain, arms, legs, body to serve the World and Humanity by accomplishing and becoming all a Human being is capable of becoming. Our ego convinced us we are our bodies and that our life belongs to us. The sooner we remember that the body belongs to the soul and return the control of the body back to the soul, the sooner our lives will be fulfilling. When we remember this fact and begin to listen to our thoughts, the thoughts and beliefs we have inherited from others, the sooner we can come in contact with the truth. To live our best life, I believe having access through intuition, through knowingness, through direct soul contact is imperative. Before we seek this and gain it, our egos are in control of our thoughts, our actions and our fears.

Soul contact happens through intention. When we begin to remember the idea that the soul created the body for its use and agree to relinquish the ego's agenda in favor of the soul's agenda, the sooner we will find true peace and happiness. Everyone is capable of soul contact. Everyone may experience soul contact differently. The highest level of soul contact is knowingness. To see spiritually is vibrationally Third and Fourth dimensional. Spiritual hearing is vibrationally fourth and the lowest part of the Fifth dimension. Most of us came into these incarnations from dimensions higher than the fourth dimension. Most of us came from the higher Fifth dimension or even higher. Our souls do not want us to vibrationally retard ourselves to spiritual seeing, spiritual hearing; they are waiting for us to ask for knowingness. Your knowingness may be so strong that it registers in every sense of your body and may seem as if you saw, as if you heard, as if you felt with your hands what comes to you in knowingness.

When we begin to listen to ourselves and to sort through our fears and erroneous beliefs, when we agree to turn our will back to the soul, it doesn't mean we forfeit our free will. Our Freewill is a gift from God. Our lives were meant to be co-creative lives between the soul and the body. In searching for what it is we truly love, we will also discover what our soul loves. Living our best lives will also be living the life we were created to live.

We will find out by listening to our thoughts why we may feel undeserving, unworthy, not intelligent enough, not educated enough to be a success in life. Once we check our thinking and our beliefs about ourselves, we can see why we have settled for living little lives. Only you can evaluate your progress. It is important to train yourself to be your own authority to be self-administered. It is important to observe and to experiment in life. In observing ourselves closely and observing other people we gain greater understanding of what is true, what is real, what is illusion, and what we've been taught that isn't true. Our goal and the goal of our souls is for us to self-actualize, to make the most of ourselves, to become all we are capable of being. We do not serve ourselves or the World by thinking and acting small.

Knowing how to get information is more important than using the mind as a storage facility for facts.

Listen to yourself, especially when you make excuses such as: why you haven't, why you don't, why you can't, or why you aren't. Many people use their health, lack of education or intelligence, lack of luck, fear, they're too old or too young, they use I don't have enough money as an excuse for not living their best life, when in actuality it is usually lazy or erroneous thinking that stops us. Or the fact that we have developed bad attitudes about ourselves and life that stops us. Too many people spend their energy worrying about what might happen, worrying about their health, worrying about money, worrying about what other people think, worrying about what the government is going to do, worrying about their family, worrying about the future to actually be fully present in their own lives.

What really matters is not how much intelligence we have, but how we use what we do have. The thinking that guides our intelligence is more important than how much intelligence we have.

**God does not choose the qualified.
God qualifies those who choose to serve.**

Become an aware person. Practice staying aware, not only of what you are thinking and feeling, but in observing what is happening all around you. Catch yourself when you get lazy and tune out from what you are thinking, feeling and what is happening around you. Commit to remaining conscious at all times.

Many people are afraid to think big, because they are under the illusion that everything is up to them. They are completely unaware that their soul is there to help them to accomplish their goals and desires. When I left banking and began to communicate with my soul I had no idea I could be an artist, a spiritual teacher and counselor. I not only didn't know I could paint, I had even less of an idea how to market what I created in writing and in painting. As I've progressed my soul has opened the way to each thing as I would trust and attempt. Much of what has happened is sometimes even difficult for me to believe, because it has been so seemingly miraculous, so synchronistic. But, each time I've followed the soul's suggestions, miraculous connections have happened.

I had a difficult time in the beginning, because I wanted the soul to be logical and efficient. I wanted the messages to be very specific and I wanted to know more than just the next single thing to do. I wanted to know the future before it happened. The soul was kind enough not to show me the future, knowing it would scare me into stopping. I finally learned the truth was I only needed to know the next thing and then the next thing and that to know more than that I would try to take over and figure out what to do rather than to continue to listen. Each time I would trust and follow the suggestions, even though I couldn't see how it had anything to do with what I considered to be my goals, amazing connections would happen. Well, that's not completely true sometimes I would follow and seemingly nothing obvious would happen. At those times Spirit would assure me that the other person didn't follow their intuition to show up. Then they would have to rearrange the scheduling so I would connect with that person another way at another time.

I think the most important thing I learned was that the messages were not orders; they were suggestions. Before I turned my life over to God, or the soul, I had fear of what I would be asked to do, of what I would be asked to give up. But, I turned my life over out of desperation and was willing to have God the soul to tell me what to do. So when the messages started coming I saw them as orders from God and attempted to do every one without question. I later got so tired and so in debt that I was ready to quit following the messages and that is when the soul explained that the messages were suggestions and not orders and that I had a right to negotiate with the soul by writing out conditions under which I could attempt what was being suggested. I was also given a method of how to get myself out of debt. While I was filling out the form I had no faith that it would cause any positive difference in my debt.

FINANCIAL CONDITION

To get a clear image of your financial condition list your current financial indebtedness or responsibilities.

                              Total Balance   Monthly Responsibility

Mortgage or Rent_____
Car Payments_____
Utilities:
Gas _____
Electric_____
Home Phone/Internet
Cable TV_____
Cell Phone_____
Water/ Sewer _____
Subscriptions _____
Bottled Water_____
Maintenance_____
Car Loans _____
Bank Loans _____
Credit Cards _____
    Capital One_____
    Chase _____
    Master Card_____
    VISA_____
    CITI_____
    American Express_____
    Discover_____
    Department Store_____
Personal Loans_____
Insurance
  Personal_____
  Medical_____
  Life_____
  Auto_____
  Renters_____
  Mortgage_____

Taxes
    State_____
    Federal_____
    Other_____

Totals:

I now release this indebtedness into the Universe. I now accept its immediate and complete payment through rich avenues of Divine Substance. I now accept being totally debt free through financial abundance. And so it is!

We continue to pay our monthly obligations to the debt we have created. The reason we ask that we become debt free through financial abundance is to not make the method we use to become debt free by committing bankruptcy. I saw no way that I was personally able to clear the debt I had created while following Spirit's suggestions to travel, but within one year I received an inheritance from a friend of $25,000 and a cash gift of $1,000.

Living our best life includes living with financial serenity, not financial security. It is important to realize that there is no such thing as financial security. Money can always be devalued by the government, stolen, miss handled by financial institutions, jobs can be taken away, retirement investments confiscated or devalued. The only security I have found is in learning the Laws of Manifestation: Desire, Intention, Belief, Anticipation or Expectancy, and Gratitude. Using the Law of Attraction I've learned that the higher I can raise my vibration the faster I can manifest my desires because like attracts like. If my vibration is high, my intention is clear and I show up, miracles happen. Spirit has taught me not to think in terms of how much a thing will cost, not to think in terms of money, but to write down the end result I desire.

In the Fourth dimension the Laws of Manifestation require that we write our desires in writing in order for there to be a contract between the body and the soul, which gives the soul permission to intervene on our behalf. At the top of each page on which you write your desires, Spirit suggests we use the following phrase: I desire, intend, deserve and now gratefully accept" followed by a detailed description of the desire. At the bottom of each page it is suggested that we release the request to the soul and the Universe with the following sentence: "I now accept this or something better, through the grace of God and to the highest good of all concerned." The top phrase includes intention, desire, expectation, acceptance in present tense and gratitude, which are all important in manifesting. The bottom phrase gives the soul permission to give us something even better than what we have been able to imagine, since, in my experience, Spirit seems to think we seldom think big enough.

In designing our lives on paper we have a tendency to become clearer about the truth of our heart's desires. I look at them as sending purchase orders into the Universe. When I was designing the location for this retreat center, I had written that the center would have a view of a large body of water. The first property I was shown was across the street from a city water tower. Spirit fortunately has a sense of humor. They were attempting to teach me to be more specific. The actual center has a view of a river.

When we continue to think in terms of how much something would cost and let ourselves use that as an excuse not to begin; we are building a fence between us and the manifestation of the desire. The soul has to knock down or go around our money fence to bring us to the desire. When we think in terms of the end result instead and leave out the cost of the object and the how it will be accomplished, opportunity or condition can appear without money being involved or at the time we will have the funds to accomplish the goal.

After a couple of years of living in the center the building needed a new roof. I had no idea how much a roof would cost, which was a good thing, because I wasn't inclined to think about affording it. I just wrote, "I now accept having a new roof on the building at no cost to me." I did know that the job would be huge, because there were wood shingles under a composition roof. Both roofs would have to be removed and plywood decking would have to be installed before a new roof could be attached. I kept my focus on the end result. I tried to stay away from thinking about the mess getting the new roof could create. A few days later a young man came to the front door and asked permission to climb onto the roof to see if he could get me a new roof. He and his crew were in town from Dallas, because there had been a recent hail storm. He took pictures of the damage and offered to go to my insurance company to negotiate the new roof. The next day he came back and said the insurance company had agreed to letting him put on the new roof at no cost to me.

My father and my brother are roofing contractors in Lubbock, Texas and I know what a mess can be made when tearing off and replacing roofs and how unscrupulous some roofers are. This young man's crew came the next day and covered the ground around the house with blue tarps and backed a dump truck into the driveway. They moved every potted plant to the back of the deck and covered the koi pond with a tarp. They accomplished the entire roof in one day, removed the tarps, replaced all the plants exactly where they had been before, ran a magnetic bar over the lawn to pick up any nails and left me with a beautiful new roof at no cost to me. It felt like magic.

When you wish to travel or to receive further education, it is also important not to think in terms of how much it would cost. It is important to write down where you would like to travel, how you would like to travel, by plane, train or automobile. It is important to accept the degree you wish to accomplish or the subject you wish to master. When my children had reached the age that they qualified to attend college I did not have the money to send them. I wrote: "I now accept being able to offer my children higher education." Within a week a man in Arizona called me and said, "Spirit is suggesting that I offer to send your children to college, what would that involve?" Even though the person was a person I knew, he was not a person I would have thought of asking to do something so huge for me. One of my children chose not to go to college. The man paid for books and tuition for the other one to go long enough to receive her Bachelors Degree.

I've learned that when the soul wishes to have my body travel somewhere that it is a good idea for me to write down conditions under which I could travel such as: A paid for plane ticket, someone fun to travel with, perfect ground transportation, perfect places to stay, perfect food to eat, perfect clothes to wear, someone who knows the language and customs of the people in the area where I will be traveling. I would suggest the same to you.

Living our best life includes being comfortable, but not so comfortable that we are not willing to change, to risk, to adjust ourselves and our circumstances. Life is about change. The earlier in our lives we get comfortable with the idea and the reality that there will always be changes and learn to change gracefully, the earlier we will feel comfortable in our bodies and in our lives. We can let life happen to us or we can deliberately participate, co-create our lives with our souls.

I write out my desires in detail in the format Spirit has suggested and I live with only one question: "What is the next single thing for me to do or know for me to be in a state of Divine Grace?" When I feel the urge, the intuition to call someone, to go to a certain place, to research a certain subject, to look on my bookshelves for a certain book, to eat at a certain restaurant at a certain time, to go to a different drug or grocery store than the one I usually go to, to write a letter or send a note to a certain person whose name comes to mind, to plan a trip or to take a nap, I make an effort to accomplish what I feel is being suggested. As a result of living this way I have found peace. I can feel I am always at the right place, at the right time, with all I was supposed to take with me. Knowing this and letting go of the fear of rejection, the fear of embarrassment, the doubt that I'm receiving the intuition correctly, the fear I'm not doing something right has brought me proof that my soul and the Universe are on my side. Usually I feel the fear and proceed in spite of the feelings of fear. I do still have difficulty asking other people to help me, but I'm working to overcome this fear.

Recently I needed all of the flowerbeds behind the center redone. I had neither the money to pay someone to do it or the physical strength to accomplish it myself. I know that action in the direction of the goal is often important. So I bought the landscaping fabric and the cedar mulch to accomplish my vision. Within a week three women who were visiting the center asked me what I intended to do with all the supplies lying on the deck and I explained my vision, my intention. They volunteered to do the labor and accomplished it in two days.

We all have talents, gifts to be shared with the world and each other. To be afraid to attempt to use these gifts doesn't serve us and it doesn't serve the World or Humanity. We are required to extend ourselves. Shyness does not serve our souls. Fear does not serve our souls. Self-doubt does not serve us or the soul. To begin to believe we live in a benevolent Universe is a big step. To think that some intelligence is behind keeping the planets in orbit, the plants, minerals and animals available for our nourishment, the Sun and Moon available for our light and heat and water available for us to drink shows me that the Universe is benevolent and desires our survival.

When we put out purchase orders in writing, the soul and the Universe begin to respond to our requests. I never cease to be amazed when other people listen to their souls and respond to their soul's request to specifically help me or to support the Namaste center. It is always reassuring to know that other people are listening to their souls and that some of them are brave enough to follow their soul's suggestions. It reassures me that I live in a benevolent Universe filled with Spirits who are communicating with Human beings.

Listening to our intuition or for messages from our souls and following those suggestions will cause us to live our best lives.

LAW OF ATTRACTION AND MAGNITISM
EVERY THOUGHT HAS CREATIVE POWER

When we focus on what we don't desire to happen, we give energy to that happening. When we focus on the lack of something that we desire, we attract more lack, rather than what we desire. In order to have what we desire, we must focus our thoughts and emotions on that which we desire with intention. Every thought is not equal in its ability to create. The more emotion behind a thought the faster the event will become physical. Therefore, it is important to realize that if we fear or dread something we are calling that event to ourselves. Repetition of thought, "habitual thought," causes creation even if there is not great emotion behind the thought. This is why it is important to look at our "habitual" thoughts. What thoughts run through our minds when we are driving, showering, shaving, putting on our makeup? What thoughts do we have when we are not deliberately thinking?

Do we repetitiously think "I want" or "I need?" If so, the sub-conscious mind takes our thoughts literally and believes we want to stay in a state of wanting or needing, since that is what we are asking for. It is important to think literally, since the sub-conscious takes our thoughts literally and works to manifest what we are thinking and imagining. Therefore, it would be more prudent to think "I desire intend, deserve and now gratefully accept," rather than to think need, want or to think about what you lack. We often think we are ready to have something, such as a relationship, when in actuality we have conflicting emotions and thoughts about how having a relationship would change our lives. Being ready to accept what you ask for is extremely important. If we ask for something and it appears in our lives, but appears through a source that we don't desire to receive from or through, we can deny the manifestation, believing that God does not know the best way for us to get what we are asking for. This is why it is useful at the bottom of each page of writing out your intentions and desires to place this affirmation:

"I now accept this or something better, through the grace of God and to the highest good of all concerned."

We do not always know what is to our highest good. We don't always think big enough or expansive enough. We don't always understand why a certain person would be sent to help or to serve us. If we use this affirmation, we can trust that the situations we manifest will be "win/win" for all parties concerned.

It is important to have dominant intentions about our lives. If it is our dominant intention to be healthy, wealthy, wise and to have physical, mental and emotional clarity at all times, we are much more likely to have a happy life than if we are filled with doubt, fear, guilt, jealousy, resentment, and greed. It is also important not to get caught up in trying to figure out the "how" a thing could or will happen. In doing this, we have a tendency to miss create. Leave the "how" to God.

MANIFESTING RELATIONSHIPS

When I first learned about "thoughts are things" and how to manifest what you desire in your life, I began to keep a manifestation journal. This book contains lists of desires I wish to manifest in my life. I had been through three marriages and divorces so I wasn't ready to take on another permanent, live-in, promise to be with you forever relationship. I was homeless at the time and traveling with only the belongings that would fit in my car, but I was lonely. I knew that I was totally committed to do hourly, whatever my spiritual guidance suggested and I knew that a relationship could complicate that commitment. But I also believed that **God is infinitely creative** and could come up with a relationship that would work with my current lifestyle.

I wrote out a decree stating that "I now accept a relationship with a male who is not married, who is available, has no ex-wives or children. He is sexual, sensual, romantic and adventurous. He must be healthy and willing to be monogamous for the duration of our relationship. He must be willing to travel to be with me once a month for a four day "honeymoon," wherever God has sent me at that time. He must be willing and able emotionally and financially to fly himself to that location. He will bring champagne, flowers, milk chocolate, massage oil and a willingness to eat at wonderful restaurants. He will make the plane reservations and reservations at beautiful resorts and hotels. He has his own life and does not need me, but desires to love and cherish me and to be loved and appreciated during the time we have together."

At the time I made this list, it was 1986. I stood on top of a picnic table in Rooster Park in the Columbia River Gorge and read the decree aloud to the Universe ending with: "I now accept this or something better, through the grace of God and to the highest good of all concerned."

During these years of traveling I did not stay in daily contact with anyone other than my Higher Self. I did, however, send notes to my children and a few friends to let them know approximately where I would be at any given time. One such friend was David, who I have mentioned before who had moved from Houston to Austin, Texas. I had told him I was on my way to Portland, OR and the number of the family I would be staying with for a few days. I arrived at their home a few hours after making the relationship decree. These people were friends of friends that I had met in Oklahoma City. When I arrived, they mentioned that a man had called and wanted to take me to breakfast the next morning. They gave me his number. I called and discovered that he was the best friend of David. David had called Robert and had asked him to entertain me while I was in Oregon. We went to have breakfast the next morning. He was unmarried (in fact, had never been married), had no children, was more or less married to his job, which caused him to travel continually. He fit all of the criteria I had listed. We spent time together during my time in Oregon and developed a relationship which led to our meeting and spending time together, just as I had imagined, for several years. It worked well for both of us until he was forced to retire from Honda against his desires and he began to drink daily.

In 1990, when I once again had a home base, I rewrote my decree. I made a list of the attributes I desired in a mate. The list contains 85 items. I've been involved in many male/female relationships in my life so I know what works for me and what doesn't. My experience has been that once we make our list, the Universe begins to send "candidates" to see if we will compromise our list.

When I made my list it did not really occur to me, at that time, the real purpose of relationships. On my list I asked to have someone who was financially independent, hoping to attract someone who would take care of me financially so I could do my spiritual work and creative work without having to figure out how to care for myself financially. **I now know that once you make your list it is important to read your list in terms of yourself and to see if you are as developed as what you are seeking in another person.** If you are not, you know where you need to begin to work on yourself. If you are married or in a relationship, <u>**do not show your list to that person**</u>. If it is to the soul's highest good, that person will begin to change to meet the list you have created.

I was living in Albuquerque in 1990, just having ended a nine month relationship in Mt. Shasta, California. Spirit sent me to Oklahoma City for an art show. During that week I met a man who was 82 of the 85 things

I had listed. To a practical person this seems almost too good to be true. Remember, the Universe will send "looks like" candidates to see if we will compromise our lists. In this case I did. I felt the match of 82 out of the 85 things I had listed was as close as I would ever hope to get to my list. Ignoring the fact that he wasn't financially independent and he had no concept of how to manage the small amounts of money he did manifest, I moved to Oklahoma City to be with him. Daily I overlooked the three things he wasn't and enjoyed the 82 things he was. I increased my ability to manifest to include covering his expenses. After three years, I began to resent the fact that he wasn't living up to his potential and that I was working more and more to make up for it. I dissolved our living arrangement.

Later, looking back at the scenario, I realize that I compromised my list because I didn't believe I deserved exactly what I was asking for and I didn't believe a male existed who was everything I had on my list. I also realized that what I did attract spiritually was exactly what I needed in a relationship to cause me to grow in the area of manifestation where I was still weak, which is the true purpose of relationships: to force us to grow.

Since 1993, I have avoided focusing on creating a primary male/female relationship, becoming aware that I do not believe it is possible for me to create something I've never seen. In March of 2005, I once again began to think about the possibilities. I confronted God with my beliefs. "I've never seen a male who is all 85 of the things I've written down. I know I can't manifest something that I don't believe exists. I can't visualize something that I've never seen. If I've never seen an aardvark I can't manifest an aardvark. How can I manifest something I've never seen?"

As so often happens for me, God's answers come through books that light up or fall off the shelves of my library. The next morning after my tirade at God, I noticed a book I haven't opened in many years called *The Path of Least Resistance* by Robert Fritz. When I opened the book I opened to a chapter that said: "If you are attempting to manifest something that you do not believe exists – STOP."

"Well, that's not going to get me what I desire," I argued.

The next paragraph stated: "Instead, write an affirmation asking to be healed of your doubt, your fear and your disbelief."

"Duhh, how come I never thought of that?"

The next morning during my meditation and study time, I wrote an affirmation asking to be healed of my doubt that such a male exists, my fear of how having such a relationship would change my life and my disbelief that my having such a relationship is possible. I suddenly remembered how quickly the Universe had previously answered my requests. So instead of asking for a person who fit all 85 of the criteria for the perfect relationship, I asked the Universe to just send an available male, someone to date who would enjoy going out to eat with me, going to the movies and maybe traveling or going to the casino with me. I had witnessed couples together at the casino who seemed to be having a fun time. One of my recent spiritual assignments has been to go to the Indian casinos and to set up a Christ Consciousness vortex in each one that will bless the Indians and the people who come to the casinos.

All day, after writing the affirmation, I felt an impulse to go to a certain casino in the evening. I resisted the message. I only go to the casino with a certain kind of entertainment, never income of the organization or income needed to keep all my financial responsibilities current. In that category of income, I had $12.00. From Oklahoma City one must drive at least an hour round trip to go to a casino. I was not willing to drive that far with only $12.00. Late in the afternoon I was at my bank cashing the $12.00 check. The inner voice prompted again, "Go to Lucky Star Casino." I finally agreed to drive there, much against my better judgment. After the first thirty minutes I was up $200 and feeling better now that I was playing with the "house's" money. I decided to leave my machine to go to the bathroom and to get a drink.

As I approached the entrance to the bathrooms a man came out and literally ran into me. He was an older gentleman and a bit shaky and unstable on his feet. He stepped back but continued to hold onto my shoulders as he looked into my eyes. I recognized him as a man I had dated in 1981, before my spiritual communication started. We were both astonished to be running into each other (literally) after twenty plus years. He was so emotionally moved by the encounter that he had tears in his eyes. He held onto me and whispered questions into my ear. He had developed Parkinson's disease, which caused him to whisper and not to be stable when walking. He asked if I was married or in a relationship and if I was now living in Oklahoma City. He was neither married nor in a current relationship. He was thrilled we had reconnected. I immediately realized how I had compromised my list. He was male, available, would love to go out to eat with me, to the movies, to travel, and we were meeting in a casino. I all but slapped myself for ignoring the Law of Manifestation. I knew better.

When I was 40, someone twelve years older than me did not seem old. At the age of 64, someone 12 years older than me with Parkinson's seemed really old.

One of my other "beliefs," born of experience with men, is that their primary thoughts in relationship to women are sexual. Within the first three minutes of my re-meeting this man, who can barely walk across a room and barely talk, he looked me in the eye and said, "You know I finally got rid of that bed." I could hardly believe it, in his condition it took him less than three minutes to think of me in his bed! I gave him my card and asked him to call me so we could meet in a quieter place to catch up on what had transpired in the past twenty plus years. I knew the meeting had significance and had been arranged by our souls. As soon as I had given him my card and we had parted, I felt as if I energetically had a ball and chain around my ankle. I could feel him thinking about me, wondering when we would get together and what it would be like.

In Oklahoma, we have a free paper called the *Gazette*. In this paper, there is a horoscope written by a man in California who is very intellectual, very amusing and very accurate. The week of April first he prints a funny April fool's horoscope for each sign and then under it he writes the real one. The week after this meeting, I read my horoscope. "God noticed you crying in your pillow because he hasn't sent your soul mate. I'm sorry to report God misunderstood and thought you said "cell mate." The real horoscope for that week was, "Write the book you would want to read yourself."

Be careful what you ask for and how you ask. Be sure you are ready. Read your list for your potential partner and see if you are as developed as what you are asking for. The most important thing I've learned in listening and following my soul is to keep my sense of humor. I highly recommend it.

The best affirmation I've ever read for attracting a relationship is from Julia Cameron in her book *Heart Steps*.

"**I now accept and draw to me true love...**
I draw to myself my right partner,
The soul whose love serves my soul's highest potential,
The soul whom my soul enhances to its highest potential.
I draw this partner to me freely and lovingly.
As I am drawn to this partner
I choose and am chosen out of pure love,
Pure respect and pure liberty.
I attract one who attracts me equally.
I seek and am found.
We are a match made in heaven to better this Earth."

May you be blessed with relationships that will cause you to grow spiritually through joy, love and adventure.

MANIFESTING AUTOMOBILES

When I left Texas in 1979 to move to Oklahoma City, I had a beautiful yellow, 1977 Buick. I had never had the responsibility of maintaining a car, since my husband owned an automotive garage, so I had no knowledge of how to take care of a car. Within two years the car was using more oil than it was gas and was mortgaged for more than it was worth.

In May of 1985 I was asked one morning in meditation by Spirit to sell the greeting card company that I had been using as my means of income. It sold the same day (the full story was in a previous paragraph). It was suggested that I sell all my belongings except my car, clothes and a few books, because I was going to begin to travel. I was told that each day I would be told where to go and the names of the people I was to find. I couldn't imagine traveling in the car I had. Spirit suggested that I buy a new car. They suggested that it was blue and had five doors and would get 30 miles to a gallon of gas.

When I sold the greeting card company I had used the money to pay off my credit cards. I had no visible means of income. My car was not in good condition and was financed for more than it was worth. The idea of buying a new car seemed preposterous to my logic. I went to a couple of dealers and each time the salesmen were rude and told me I couldn't afford a new car. That week my son broke out in chicken pox. Needless to say, I felt stymied and confused. I yelled at God that if He wanted me to have a new car that He would have to have it delivered to my driveway; I was not going back to any more car lots to be dismissed by anymore males. (Tremendous emotion went out with this request.) That day, a letter came in the mail from one of the dealerships I had visited. The dealership had just been purchased by a new owner. The letter was from the new owner who said he had noticed from their records that I had visited his dealership but I had not bought a car and he personally wanted to know why they had not been able to assist me.

I called his personal number and gave him an earful of how rude his salesman had been to me. I explained that after checking the condition of my car and employment that he had dropped me off at the used car lot without even introducing me to a used car salesperson. The owner was extremely apologetic. He asked me what kind of vehicle I was looking to purchase. I gave him the description that Spirit had given me. The part about five doors was still confusing to me. I had never had a car with a hatchback, so had never considered this as a fifth door. He replied that he had that exact car in his show room and he would personally be glad to show it to me. I explained to him that my son had chicken pox and that it would be a few days before I could go out again to look at cars and that I was now considering another brand. He asked me what kind of payment I thought I could manage. Out of my mouth came, "$200." Since I now had no income I thought I was lying. He thanked me and hung up.

Twenty minutes later the original salesperson who had been so rude to me called. He apologized and said, "I don't know what you said to Mr. Smicklas, but he has instructed me to bring the car and the contract to your house as soon as it is convenient for you." He brought the car and contract. I signed it and he took away my damaged car. The contract included the dealership paying off the bank note I had on my old car. I drove this car for three years from one side of the United States to another and back again. When I began to travel, I thought it would be for the three months of the summer and then I would rent another house and the children would come back to live with me. Spirit had another idea. The children chose to stay with their Dad in Texas and Spirit asked me to continue to travel. The truth was, if I was going to continue to travel and live out of my car, I now needed a van, rather than a hatchback.

I wrote out my intention to now accept a blue minivan, with cruise control, cassette player and electric windows, doors and seats. I still had no visible means of income. Shortly after writing my desire and intention, I was traveling through Amarillo, Texas, and stopped to visit with a woman I had previously met there. I did not mention to her my desire to have a van, but while we were visiting she said, "You know, bj, if you are going to continue to travel I think you need to get a minivan." I laughed and told her I agreed with her but that I did not see how, short of a miracle, that it could happen. She pointed out that her father always bought his cars from this one dealer in Pampa, Texas, and she thought if we went to see him, he could help me. Of course she didn't say "father" she said "My Daddy" with a southern drawl. We drove to Pampa and she explained to the dealer that I was a friend of her "Daddy" (who I've never met) and that I needed a minivan. The man did not hesitate; he did not ask about my income, he did not ask how much I owed on the car I was driving. He simply said, "Do you see anything you like?"

I pointed to a blue Ford minivan. He asked if I would like to drive it first. My friend and I drove the car around for a few minutes. All the time we are driving I was in doubt that this could happen, because I had no proof of employment and I was still what is known in the car business as "upside down" in my present car (meaning I still owed more than the car was worth.) When we got back to the lot the owner took us inside to his office. He asked a few questions about where the car I was driving was financed. He filled out the papers himself and made a call to Ford Motor Credit to assure the financing. I signed the papers and drove away in the van. Trading cars, or buying a new vehicle, has always been one of my least favorite things to do. The van I've been driving now has over 100,000 miles on it and it is time to trade up. The car knows this. A friend just backed into the side of it as she was leaving the driveway. I'm expecting another miracle.

Next time I needed to change cars I took my attorney with me for support. I knew exactly what Spirit had suggested as the next best choice for me. It was a Subaru Forrester. I knew the color was to be silver or platinum and all the accessories I desired. I also knew that buying the outgoing model rather than the newest model would save me several thousand dollars.

When a salesman approached us, I asked to be taken to the finance officer's office. The officer asked me what kind of vehicle I was looking for. I told him the details and he started typing on his computer to look at their inventory. He said he only had one 2017 Forrester left and it was the color of the one I had described, which seemed to surprise him. He worked to get the car financed, which I knew might be difficult, because my name is on my daughter's mortgage. She became unemployed and her mortgage is not current. I was not notified of the arrears until I did not have the funds to bring it current. The rest of my credit score is in the 700, but as usual, I stated mentally that I expected a positive exception to be made in my favor.

He called me and told me he was able to get the car financed through Tinker Credit Union. They called him the next day and cancelled their willingness to accept the responsibility. He called and told me not to worry that he would find a way. He continued to be tenacious on my behalf and finally got the financing through the Oklahoma Teacher's Credit Union.

One of our main problems as Humans is our logic. Because of mass consciousness belief, our logic will create reasons why miracles can't happen for us. We have a tendency to believe that no matter what we want to do, the money has to come first. We are stuck in thinking in terms of money instead of thinking in terms of energy. We came to Earth to prove direct manifestation, to bring Spirit into matter. When we think of a desire, ordinarily, our left brain will put a price tag on the desire. We are being asked by our souls to begin to think beyond money. We are being asked to go directly to the desire, to think energetically. Raising our own personal vibration and stating our intentions clearly, with a willingness to accept what we desire through whatever means our soul chooses to use to gift us with our desire, is our challenge.

Our first job is to be clear about what we desire and to be clear energetically from doubt, fear and disbelief. Be clear about what is our true heart's desire. Don't ask for what you want or need; ask for your true heart's desire.

MANIFESTING EMPLOYMENT

The single most important thing about asking for employment is to not see your employment as the source of your supply. Your employment is to be your service to Humanity, the Universe and your soul. For the masses, employment equals income. Truly our employment is to be our means of soul growth. It brings us in contact with the people our soul feels would bring us the most growth. We are to choose something we truly love to do in order that our service is truly inspired. Even if you are retired (Spirit prefers that we think of retirement as a graduation) it is important to have some form of service that we perform.

List what you love to do – not thinking about "how will this make me a living." We are not creative enough to think up a job or service to match all of our talents. We are too stuck in the money aspect of employment. There are so many jobs and opportunities out there that we've never heard of or thought of. God is infinitely creative.

Years ago it was time for my children to go to college and I didn't have the money and their Dad had not created savings for this. I wrote in my manifestation journal, "I now accept being able to offer my children higher education." Within a few days a friend in Arizona called and said he had received in meditation that he was to offer higher education to my children and asked what that involved. My daughter accepted his offer and entered college; my son decided not to go to college. While my daughter was in college she became engaged to be married. Then, suddenly, the groom decided that he would not be good husband material and backed out of the marriage. Shortly, thereafter, my daughter found she was pregnant. She was working as a bartender. The situation seemed overwhelming to both of us. But we sat down and focused on what she really desired. We wrote about her new job with conditions that seemed would be impossible to fulfill even for God.

She needed a new car. We asked that the new job would pay mileage so that she could get a new car. We asked that the job would pay at least $10.00 per hour. Minimum wage at this time was at something just over $5.00. We knew the job would be part time, so that she could continue to go to school, but we also asked for medical benefits for herself and the baby. We asked that she could make her own hours and, if it became necessary, that she could take the baby to work with her. We asked that she could work from home. We asked that she could fulfill this job without having to buy a new wardrobe. Our requests seemed impossible, but we had faith that she was doing what her soul intended and that she and the baby would be taken care of. I agreed to quit traveling for two years to be the baby's nanny.

Within a few short days she received a call from a neighbor of the mother of the baby's father. This person stated that he did not feel that the father was living up to his responsibility and that he wanted to help. He asked her about her intended employment. He knew she had been working as a bartender, because he had hired her to serve as a bartender for some of his backyard parties. He proposed that he would call a company that his company distributed for and ask them to create a position that he felt she would be perfect for. The position would be one of being a liaison between his company and the company they distributed for. He explained that the majority of the work would be for her to drive to each of the fifteen Wal-Mart stores in the Oklahoma City area to only straighten the Edy's ice cream. This job did not involve delivering the ice cream, only in keeping the display straightened twice a week. My daughter is a Virgo; keeping order is one of her most natural skills. He made the call to his connection within the other company and she did not even have to be interviewed. She had the job. They agreed to pay her $10.00 an hour plus mileage. The stores are open 24 hours a day and she could go anytime they were open and, if necessary, take the baby in the grocery cart when she went into each store. They gave her a computer, fax and paid for her cell phone.

We did not know such a job existed; actually it didn't exist until she described it. The Universe created if for her out of our desires. She did not see the job as the source of her supply, she continued to affirm: God is the Source of my Supply. The medical benefits were provided from other sources and other sources of income came to her. All the needs of the baby were fulfilled. The baby's father is a good father. He has the child every other weekend. When she received her Bachelor's Degree, the company hired her as a full time employee with all benefits.

If we see our employment as the source, God can only send us what will fit through our paycheck. If we see our work as our "service to the Universe" and continue to see God as the Source of our supply, we leave open several billion other directions from which our supply can come.

If we truly understand who we are by this definition: "I AM God operating through my personality for the benefit of Earth, all species of life on the Earth and beyond," we can begin to think differently. And, <u>as we think, so shall our life become</u>.

In our lives we will often find situations where it is difficult to converse with certain people. I've learned from Spirit that a problem can never be solved at the energetic level it was created. When I had trouble with this, my soul gave me a method whereby I would write letters to the Oversoul and Guardian Angel. I've used it successfully several times; once when my grown son came to live with me. He was still drinking beer and smoking pot and his room was a pit. I had recently read a book about Fung Shui, which showed that the room he was living in was the direction from which prosperity was to come into my life. I didn't feel comfortable kicking him out. I wrote the letters asking that he would find a place he would rather be. I didn't get past the fourth day of writing when he came home and said, "Mom, I know you may feel like I'm abandoning you, but I have found this place I think I would rather be."

He had met a young man who was moving to China for ten years. The man had just inherited a run down two bedrooms, one bath home from his grandfather and he didn't want to leave it empty. He gave my son a ten year lease at $175.00 a month, with the proviso that he would fix it up.

In another situation, my next door neighbor died and her grown daughter moved her children and all her grandchildren along with all their dogs into the home. It was a disaster for me. I could no longer be comfortable in my front or backyard because of the noise and the children wanting to play in my front yard. I wrote the letters asking the daughter's soul to find another place she would rather be. Shortly thereafter, she took the equity out of the house, then let it go into foreclosure, moved to the country and built a metal building for them all to live in. I now have great peaceful, helpful, quiet neighbors living next door.

LETTER WRITING TO THE OVERSOUL AND GUARDIAN ANGEL

You may use this method if you have a situation that needs healing, a condition you cannot resolve or a person with whom you have no luck communicating in the Third dimension. This creates no negative karma. You are allowed to write a letter similar to the one that follows. Writing and burning the letters when you have 14 letters gives the persons' soul permission to over ride their free will for six weeks to help them.

To the Oversoul and Guardian Angels of ___(name)_____:
I ask for Divine intervention for (my relationship with) (healing for) (the current situation for)_____(name)_____. I ask for healing of body, mind, Spirit and emotion in all dimensions and time frames. Recognizing that I do not fully understand the karmic implications in this situation, I ask the Oversoul and Angels to intervene. I ask for healing from addiction, anger, disease, (etc.). I ask that _____(name)_____ become aware of their true nature, their mission and their Oversoul. It has been promised that if we ask, we shall receive. I recognize that by writing these letters for 14 days, and on the 14th day burning the letters, I am acting in accordance with Spiritual Law. I now release this person and their condition to God for resolution. And so it is.

This method is the only way for the Oversoul and Guardian Angels to be given a special dispensation to override the person's free will for six weeks to positively influence the person's life. You may do this for addicted individuals, but the exorcism would work best for addiction as most addicted people are periodically possessed and not fighting their addiction for only one person.

This is one of the greatest gifts you can offer another person. You do not have to have their permission to write these letters. You can also write the letters for the Earth or a country, or condition which is present on the Earth.

Write the letters for 14 days. If you miss a day, keep writing until you have 14 letters. When you burn the letters, you release the person to God and ask for the highest good for all concerned. Fire energy assists in transmuting the situation. You may write the letters every 8 weeks, leaving 6 weeks in between to allow the Oversoul to intervene. Many miracles have been reported through the use of this prayer technique. Read your letter and ask yourself if you are doing this out of love for the person or because of your need to control and, if so, redo the wording of the letter and be honest about your motives.

We are now living in the Fourth dimension, which Christians would think of as hell. Earth and Humanity are on our way to the Fifth dimension, which Christians would think of as heaven. The Fourth dimension is filled with all the negative thought forms that Humans have expressed since the late 1930's. When Humans decided to attempt to split the atom, the Spiritual Hierarchy intervened and created an energetic barrier out beyond the fourth dimension to keep the effects of the chain reaction of splitting an atom from going on out to destroy the Universe. We are living in an embryonic sack of our own ca-ca. The beings that have died in a state of addiction, or with such a low frequency of energy that they could not make it through the barrier into the fifth dimension are stuck in this dimension with us. This is the reason we see so much addiction. These beings no longer have bodies through which to feed their addictions of drugs, food, sex, power, alcohol, nicotine, etc. The only relief they can get is to attach themselves to the bodies of people who are practicing their drug of choice. Many people are now possessed by these entities. It is very difficult to overcome an addiction when a person is possessed by an entity encouraging them to continue the addiction. Spirit has given the following prayer that we have permission to use to do an exorcism. You do not have to have the person's permission nor do you have to be in their presence in order to perform an exorcism, because possession is against spiritual law.

PRAYER OF EXORCISM

Through the authority vested in me by the Cosmic Christ Consciousness, I deliberately call forth to the energy of the Archangel Michael and the Band of Mercy (*a group of angels whose job it is to move lost souls out of the astral plane*) **to enter the body, home, automobile and place of work of ____(name)___ to remove all negative influences and entities. I ask that these energies and entities be taken into the Light for transmutation and that there be no negative side effects (physical, mental or emotional) to _____'s body. I ask that her/his body now be triple sealed** (*it is helpful to think of the person in three bubbles of Light – Purple, Pink and White*) **against any further invasions of negative forces.**

You may or may not choose to tone the sound OM or AUM at this point to increase the positive energy around you. Amen, Amen, Amen. Thank you, Thank you, Thank you.

BECOMING A SOUL-INFUSED PERSONALITY

A stream of Light connects us to our souls. Some refer to this as the silver cord. It is possible to deliberately increase the size of this cord and to create a bridge into space where we can go for healing or we can invite the etheric body of another to join us on this bridge to create healing in a relationship. This bridge is built through intention. Between our consciousness and the consciousness available from our soul there are magnetic streams of Light. In the back of the neck of the Human species there are seven tensor receptors. These receptors were included in the original matrix of the Homo sapiens. In most Humans I've met, these receptors are not turned on or lit up. When they are dormant it is more difficult to perceive information from our souls. Once we become aware these receptors exist we can activate them through intention during meditation or they can be activated for us by an authorized activator, which I AM. They operate similarly to crystal chips in the original crystal radios we made as children; well, maybe you didn't because you are probably not as old as I AM. We do not have to understand the inside of a radio or television in order to receive information through it. We do need to know how to turn it on and to tune it to the station we desire to pick up. The connections to our soul work in the same way as a radio would pick up transmissions. We do need to be clear what channel, frequency or station we wish to receive. All spiritual growth and manifestation happens through intention. I suggest asking to connect to the highest level of your Oversoul that your physical body can easily tolerate, through the vibration of the Cosmic Christ Consciousness.

I believe it helps to know that these receptors exist in order that we can go into meditation and turn them on. We also have the opportunity to activate three additional chakras in our bodies that will more strongly connect the body with the soul and make it easier for the soul to use the body for the purpose it was created. These three chakras are located as follows: One at the base of the skull is referred to as the "well of dreams chakra"; two is located in the roof of the mouth and is referred to as "the mouth of God chakra," (when activated, this one makes it easier for the soul to speak through the body when it is appropriate); the third is referred to as "the high heart chakra" and is located near the sternum and extends through the body to just below the heart in the back of the body. It corresponds to the opening through which the etheric form leaves the body to have out of body experiences while we are sleeping or can be accomplished through intention when we are meditating. Some people bring spiritual secrets with them from other lifetimes. These secrets are stored in the knees. I am aware when this is true for a client and get down on the floor and tone into the client's knees to break up the capsule of information, which then goes into their blood stream as consciousness.

When we first come to Earth, the silver cord is minimal and enough energy comes from the soul to keep the infant bodies functioning. As the Human body grows, more energy is given from the soul. By the time the Human body is approximately six to seven years old, much of the soul is connected to the body. At this age, many children are able to see into other dimensions and to know things before they happen in this dimension. Most of them, like most of us, were talked out of continuing to "know" or "see" things that others (grownups) did not see or know.

The amount of energy coming to the Earth at this time is tremendous. The process of enlightenment requires a well-integrated personality as a base for our Higher Self to guide us without tremendous resistance from our egos. The amount of Light flowing into our minds can and will stimulate any personality tendency, such as a sense of superiority or inferiority, or an emotion such as sadness, loneliness, grief, jealousy, possessiveness, resentment, the need to control, or anger. Your personality is working very rapidly now to integrate new circuits of reality. Our reality is rapidly changing day by day. If we attempt to live in the World today with the personality we developed twenty years ago, we will be suffering. All of us must spend some time in the presence of people who seem to be stuck in the past. We can observe how afraid or angry this makes them. They do not understand that energy is bombarding them and intensifying their personality traits. To be in public and not get caught up in their fray, it is important to stay connected to our souls, to keep our sense of humor and to remember being in a hurry screws up divine timing.

Think of the analogy of us coming to Earth and we are riding in the back seat of a shiny limo. God is driving the limo and we are happy to have the window down between the front and rear seat. At about the age of sixteen, when we get our driver's license, we decide we want to be the driver of our lives and we no longer want to take orders or suggestions from anyone. Between sixteen and twenty we think we know everything; obviously, we know more than our parents. ☺ We put God in the back seat and roll up the window between the front and back and we proceed to make trouble for ourselves. Only when we get lost or desperate do we roll the window down (pray) and ask God to help us out of some mess we have gotten ourselves into. Usually later in life (more so now for many people), we are remembering that we were supposed to be co-creators of our lives. This was supposed to be a joint effort. God sent us down here for a purpose. That purpose involved our continuing to have constant communication with that which sent us. Our purpose is to bring more and higher vibrational energy into this dimension. In an ideal situation we get out of the limo, we invite God to once again take on the driver's seat responsibilities and we get in the back seat or the observers position where we were intended to ride. The intention also is to keep the window down between the front and rear seats; to have a constant communication with God, your soul, or whatever you perceive is who sent you here.

Letting God or your soul be the driver does not in any way mean that you are a pawn and that you are to do everything that is suggested by the soul. You always maintain your free will. God or your soul will not override your free will. Suggestions will be made by God or your soul. You are free to consider whether or not you are willing to do what is suggested. If a suggestion seems scary or unclear, it is your responsibility to ask for clarification or to write down conditions under which you would take on the task. If, after you have written down your conditions you begin to see the Universe fulfill your conditions, you are then more obligated to follow through with what the soul has suggested. Some people have accused me of arguing with my soul. I would rather use the term negotiating. In one of the first messages I ever received from Spirit, I was told. "Our will for our life in you will very closely parallel your own true desires, but you must write down your desires. There will always be a way to fulfill your purpose and to enjoy your life."

Most of our problems are created by our ego ruling our personality. If we don't think of ourselves as good enough, pretty enough, strong enough, smart enough, we have a tendency to be inauthentic in our behavior. In each situation, if we continually increase the stream of energy coming into the body from the soul and invite continuous participation from the soul into the personality and the body, our lives will change. At first it may feel awful as each inappropriate personality trait comes to the fore and a circumstance will occur to bring it to our attention. We can choose how to respond now and not just come from reaction. We can become the observer, the designer, the co-creator of lives that fulfill the purpose for which we came to Earth and fulfill our Human desires simultaneously.

An example would be if I receive in meditation that the soul would like the body to be in Santa Fe in two days, I dialog and ask if we can stop in Amarillo along the way and have dinner with a dear friend that lives there and if we can drop down to Lubbock and see my niece and my two grand-nephews on the return to Oklahoma City. I also ask for the perfect place to stay in Santa Fe. After I've written my "suggestions or conditions", it would not be unusual for me to receive a call from someone who is also going to be in Santa Fe and wants to share a hotel room, or someone I know there will call and ask if I'm going to be in the area any time soon. I will get the "feeling" from my soul that stopping in Amarillo will not deter the mission of getting to Santa Fe and my friend in Amarillo will be home when I call to invite her to dinner. When I leave on the trip to Santa Fe, I may have no idea of what the mission will entail or who I will meet there. My job is to be willing, to show up and to look good. The look good part does not come from my ego. My soul is very clear that how we look determines other's first impressions of us and that, in order for that impression to be positive so the energy moves through us to them, we need to be well groomed.

When I first started working toward becoming a soul infused personality, I carried tremendous anger and sadness in my psyche and body. I was all about being "reactive" to every situation rather than understanding that the purpose of every encounter was to give me an opportunity to allow the soul to "respond" to the situation rather than for me to "react" from my accumulated pain and misconception of how the Universe works. I lived in a defensive posture. I had to be willing to get in the back seat and watch myself, my feelings, my thoughts and to wait before I spoke or acted. The first step in spiritual maturity is to begin to be aware of our thoughts in order to change them to be in alignment with the soul.

I lived in a place of continual melancholy that often moved into depression. I could not see the joy or humor in everyday occurrences, nor was I attuned to the beauty of nature. I was stuck in my preprogramming from childhood. It took years of watching myself and listening to myself to hear why I would react to certain situations in an unreasonable manner. When I began to change, it confused the people who were used to me being a certain way. When I began to live from my intuitive guidance, I was thought to be crazy by my family and friends. My husband at the time actually had me interviewed by three psychologists in an attempt to prove I was insane or emotionally unstable in order to have me committed. (In Texas, if a husband can get three psychologists to agree that a wife is unstable he can get her committed.) Frequently, our changing threatens the reality of those around us, especially those who are not willing to change or to perceive a broader reality than the one they've always known and trusted, even though it may be based on lies or inaccurate information. Many people are simply afraid to experience a fuller revelation of who they are at this time, and their fear may be projected onto you as a concern about your sanity. Instead of defending your beliefs, send them a silent blessing and move on. Your life may seem to be getting crazier at first when you begin to seek your own truth rather than your life seeming to immediately be easier. You may feel overwhelmed at first with how to integrate all the new ideas and understanding you've gained.

Staying grounded while constantly agreeing to funnel more and more Light into this dimension is extremely important. If you do not currently have a grounding process that works for you, you may go to our web site or blog and read the article on Overcoming being Empathic in Favor of Being Consciously Multi-Dimensional. The web site is: NamasteConsciousness.org the blog address is: NamasteConsciousness.com

The degree to which people hold onto those things that are not of the higher vibration is the degree to which they will experience pain. Misunderstandings and hurts from the past will be surfacing to be healed. Handling what one is accustomed to can seem easier than change. But we are at a point in evolution and energy that is extreme. Nothing happens halfway now, everything is accelerated.

I'm not a fan of astrology, since I've never studied it and don't really understand the language, but every year (once I had made contact with my soul) my soul would suggest that I have a chart and tape done by a wonderful woman who used to live in Oklahoma and now lives in Connecticut. Every year the message would be the same: "You must surrender more." Now, considering that I had surrendered my positions in the church and community, surrendered my security of having a husband, surrendered having a home of my own, had surrendered to go anywhere, do anything, say anything the soul asked of me, you might imagine this message infuriated me. I had no idea what else I could surrender. I had surrendered my body to be used by the soul. At the end of each year, I would take stock of what I had learned and realized gradually what I needed to surrender many times was "the need to know" the need to know beforehand how a situation was going to turn out, the need to know why Spirit wanted my body in Denver or Portland or Santa Fe before I would take the body there. The need to know "why" very often slowed down my progress. Each year I learned to surrender more fear, more resistance, more need to know. The more I surrendered, the more I was allowed to know.

You may want to consider your own personality. What makes you angry? What makes you sad? What makes you happy? What causes you to laugh? What scares you? Asking yourself these questions can also help you to identify your life's purpose. Once we truly understand that we are not our bodies, but are spiritual beings having this Human experience and that this experience was designed to be co-creative and fun, we can let go of much of what we have feared. The ego likes recognition. If we recognize it and give it a say in decisions, but do not allow it to rule our personality, it usually embarrasses us less often and more often we can learn to laugh at ourselves.

Getting all "het" up (that's a Texas expression meaning heated) about politics, the environment, what other people are doing, the state of the World, what your child, mother, spouse or significant other is doing or not doing is all about the ego and is a diversion from what we are to be about. When we are in a state of anger, agitation, disagreement or depression about a situation, we are not in alignment with our soul. We are not letting God drive the limo and it will make us miserable. If only things were different, then I could be happy. Things will not be different until we see them differently. If we look at the big picture of where the World and Humanity are compared to 100 years ago we can see progress.

If we look only at what's wrong, or what we perceive to be wrong, we get more of what we think is wrong. The only way to correct a situation is by looking at our perception of the situation. Other people will never please us 100% of the time. We have a responsibility to ask our souls to show us the big picture. If we look at one small part of what we think is happening on the planet and begin to judge and believe it should be different than it is, we become a part of the problem. We give our energy to the horrors we hear on the BBC news in the middle of the night or the ten o'clock news just before we go to bed. Listening to the news while riding to work, if we believe what is being reported should be other than what it is, it can ruin our whole day, our whole outlook.

We have a responsibility to focus on what's working, what's beautiful, what's good in our lives and in the World. This is not being an ostrich; it is bringing to the situation an energy that is higher than the energy that is currently operating in the circumstance. A problem can never be solved at the level of consciousness it was created. If we focus on a 3D problem with 3D energy, we expand the problem. If we focus on a 3D situation with 5D energy, we can change it or see the truth of what it is about. It is important not to ask for how to fix a problem, because it will need to be fixed again. Do not ask for an answer, because you will then have to figure out how to use the answer. Always ask for the solution which will dissolve the problem

When your spiritual body is stimulated by contact from a higher source, your personality is also stimulated. You want to be able to count on every side of your personality to use its energy to cooperate with your true life's purpose, not to sabotage your efforts and relationships.

BUILDING THE BRIDGE

There is a place that exists in another dimension of reality. It is a highly energized place that has been created by our souls and the Masters. The Higher beings of Light are focusing energy and Light on this place day and night. You may choose to see it as a Golden Pyramid, a Crystal Pyramid or a temple. Going to this place in meditation makes it possible for you to receive information from your soul, make changes in relationships, to resolve conflicts and to manifest your heart's desires.

Consider creating a personal bridge in space between you and your pyramid. Consider making the bridge up of the colors of all the Rays of energy coming from the heart of God. Let yourself intention going into meditation and going inside a Golden Pyramid. In your Golden Pyramid, you can raise the frequency of your cellular structure and heal and energize your physical body. This Pyramid is your soul in symbolic form. As you sit or lay in your Pyramid, begin to bring in each God quality and connect it to your body through the apex of the Pyramid. Bring in each quality with your breath. How you breathe strongly influences your energy field, your views and your values. Deepen your breathing and your perception changes. Thoughts become clear instead of scattered or confused. Optimistic feelings start to rise up. Your emotions tend to become calm and positive as breathing slows and the brain waves get longer. Your rhythm of breathing is important because it is a key to activating brain cells and aligning them with the frequency of your soul.

Breathe in each quality, qualities such as compassion, wisdom, love, joy, grace, beauty, courage, forgiveness, clarity, harmony, truth, trust, confidence, humor, oneness, acceptance, patience, perseverance, higher organization, a positive vision of the future, enthusiasm, serenity, understanding and peace. You may see the qualities come in as colors or you may just feel the energy. Remember, seeing is a slower form of spiritual energy, hearing is the next higher form and knowingness is an even higher form of energy. Go for the silence, go for knowingness.

Once you have established contact with your Pyramid through intention, you may take any question there and ask it of your soul. If you have someone with whom you are not in agreement, invite them silently (through intention) to join you in their etheric body in your Pyramid. At this level, have a conversation with the individual or group with whom you have trouble communicating third dimensionally. From your Pyramid you can tune the dials to the soul and send a message to any individual you wish, to a group such as the children of the World, or all of Humanity. If you do not know what message to send, you might consider this: "Live fully and in peace. Love your life. Be joyful. You are free to live from the authority of your own soul."

Communicating with someone in your Golden Pyramid does not take away their Freewill. You are inviting them into a relationship of light love. From your Pyramid you can reach anyone anywhere in the Universe. Deliberately calling forth leaders of the World into your Pyramid for conversation, to encourage loving understanding between people, even if they have different beliefs and goals, can work miracles. We have a responsibility to use all these techniques Spirit gives us to make this evolution of Earth and Humanity quicker and easier. Within the Pyramid there is no sense of time, so you can resolve conflicts that you hold in your energy field even with people who are no longer in this dimension.

Your first act of courage was to be born onto planet Earth in a Human body. Your courage to now bring in higher vibrations of energy, and to express greater wisdom and love, powerfully affects many people, including many you may never meet. True courage results in a steady and persistent intelligent action to bring about what has true value to you. <u>Each time you act with courage, you empower your entire life</u>. Every time you act from courage, you strengthen your ability to live by the authority of your own soul. And you empower others who can see the positive direction and purpose of your courage. <u>Be a living example of vitality and creativity. Courage is easier when you have a sense of real purpose</u>.

Getting in touch with your purpose for being here, beyond raising your vibration and the vibration of Earth and Humanity, is easier when you think of the things you loved to do as a child. Did you build things? Did you organize the kids in the neighborhood into a club? Did you draw on the sidewalk? Did you spend your time with a book in your face, as I did? Did you make up stories? Did you play an instrument? Did you work jigsaw puzzles? Did you throw Frisbees?

One man in a class realized that what he was good at and loved to do was to throw Frisbees. He thought of taking his skill to other countries and teaching other people to do what he loved. He got a grant from the United

Nations to make a thousand Frisbees with the emblem of the World on each disk. The grant included enough for him to make a trip to Russia to distribute the peace symbols of One World, One People, and gave him an opportunity to interact with people of a different culture doing something fun. His love of playing Frisbee caused him to become a peace ambassador. What do you love?

Take time to think; don't fill your hours with sound and activity that override your ability to hear your thoughts. What you think creates the quality of your life. If you listen to the radio, television, or other people, your quality of life is influenced by people who normally do not have your highest good in mind. They ether want to sell you something, want you to join with them in some kind of activity that is against something or want you to vote to give "them" more power. Make sure you are the one using your mind. Your mind is your most precious gift. Your mind and what you put into it creates your reality. Spend time in your Golden Pyramid. Invite scholars, inventors, composers, artists from the past whom you admire, to join you there. Ask their advice. They will join you and they will help you. All of the Masters of the Renaissance are now available to help us through this difficult period. We have access to so much help if we remember to ask.

8.

Attracting the Life We Desire

All things are constructed of atoms, from our bodies to the Solar System. You can call it magnetism, polarity, electricity, moving intelligence or God. It is everywhere. The thing that causes this energy to take physical form is thought. By changing our thoughts and beliefs, we can set up an entirely new field of magnetism within and around our bodies to attract those things we have been repelling previously by fear, limited thoughts or negative thinking.

Our Conscious Mind is the master. Our Sub-conscious Mind is the servant; it takes what we think and believe, literally, and creates it in our lives. Even if we say things in jest such as, "I feel like I've been run over by a truck" or something like "that breaks my heart," we are inviting disaster because our Sub-conscious Mind will quickly make an effort to create what we have described.

The Conscious Mind has compartments of memory, reason and imagination. The Conscious Mind exists at the level of the five senses and is quite logically a product of hearing, seeing, smelling, feeling and tasting. Its pursuit is to satisfy each of these five senses with sensations that provide pleasure instead of pain. The Conscious Mind is a pleasure and pain distinguisher and its compartment of memory, reason and imagination are but names given to its total instinct to find pleasure and avoid pain. We are endowed with the life urge to survive.

The Conscious Mind is a recorder, an analyzer and a filer. It records sensation at a level of pain and pleasure; it analyzes this sensation according to circumstances which caused it; and it files such sensation away under one of two main compartments headed "Recall about Pain" and "Recall about

Pleasure." Of itself, the Conscious Mind has no memory. In other words, it does not contain a storehouse other than what is connected to experience and sensation. The faculty of memory as applied to the Conscious Mind is simply its ability to recall certain experiences that have been recorded in the Sub-conscious Mind. If we want to remember something for easy recall, it is useful to intend it to be remembered in the short term memory of the Conscious Mind, to verbally suggest to yourself at the time that you intend to remember.

The memory of the Sub-conscious Mind is perfect. Every thought of the Conscious Mind has been indelibly recorded in the Sub-conscious as well as every sensory perception of the individual. The great mass of this material is forever lost to the recall of the Conscious Mind, for it can only be so recalled when it has previously been filed away with instructions to the Sub-conscious Mind to release it for recall. Most of it is not available to our recall.

We have within our Sub-conscious Minds, many stored thoughts and beliefs that we have accepted from mass consciousness and from what we have been taught. Much of what is in our sub-conscious is not true and no longer serves us to our highest good. The only way to reverse a negative belief or thought form is by replacing it with truth, by affirming what is true and what we do desire to believe and attract.

We create ourselves anew in every moment. This allows us to decide what type of person we want to be and make the appropriate choices. Circumstances don't determine who we are and what we become. We do. Each of us creates ourselves however we want. Regardless of what well-meaning authority figures may have told us, we can be, do or have whatever we can conceive and intend. We always have the ability to shape who we are and how we show up.

We are designed to be powerful. We can only use this unique power when we embrace the spirit within us. Without our connection to that inner power, no amount of worldly power can make a difference. With it, it is the only thing that can, not only make us feel secure or powerful, but also make us feel peaceful. There is no lasting security in machines, electricity, electronics, atomic power or money that is equal to the security one feels when they are consciously connected to their soul, their Source.

We are Spirit. We are the essence of the mighty intelligence that guides and controls the Universe. This intelligence is ours to use as we see fit. It is God-given, a divine birthright and is denied to no Human unless it is ignored and refused. There is only one mover in all creation and that mover is thought. There is only one Creator and that Creator is the Universal Superconscious Mind, or God. This Superconscious Mind creates for us exactly what we think and believe.

There is cause, there is reason, there is a power greater than we are of which we are a part. We can use this power to a make our lives good or we can ignore it and attempt to use our own power and struggle.

We are born free. Every Human is born free to discover our destiny, free to discover the Source of our being and the immensity of the spiritual power available to each of us. Thought habits of our conscious mind determine our destiny. Most Humans think habitually, repetitiously and without observing what they are thinking.

It is important for us to remember, every day of our lives, the same power that brings good fortune will also bring bad fortune and it does so according to how we use our thoughts. Without control of our thoughts, without witnessing what we are thinking, we create unconscious lives. If we use the power available to us without control, without understanding the Law of Magnetism and the Law of Attraction, and that our Sub-conscious Mind acts literally upon our thoughts we create unconsciously. Our Sub-conscious Mind is the most creative instrument in the Universe; it spans space and time, manifests form from substance, and can reach out to all knowledge. It exists in each of us. It is vitally important what we allow the Conscious Mind to feed into our Sub-conscious Mind.

We have thoughts and ideas in our Sub-conscious Mind planted by our Conscious Mind. They can be referred to as "prompters." These negative prompters have been buried in our Sub-conscious Mind very much like a forgetful dog might bury a bone and not only forget where he buried it, but also that he had buried it. We have thought things, agreed with things that are not true. These things are still buried in our Sub-conscious Minds and we are living our lives from there automatically rather than now affirming the truth and what we do desire to be our current beliefs. They can be things we heard as an infant or a small child such as "There is never enough to go around" or "People cannot be trusted."

A sick person may want to be well, but in their Sub-conscious they harbor phrases such as "there's so much sickness in the World" or "everyone is getting the flu, it's in the air," "there are so many diseases described on the TV now, how can a person be well?"

A lonely person may desire love and friends, yet in their Sub-conscious Mind they repel love by continuing to believe, "people are just out to get what they can out of me. No one can be trusted. I'm not good enough.

I'm not attractive enough. I'm not smart enough. Nobody loves me." The Sub-conscious Mind is the great creator and it creates exactly what it is prompted to create whether we remember planting these seeds or not.

We can redo these thoughts, because the Conscious Mind rules the Sub-conscious Mind. Every condition, circumstance and manifestation of our lives can be changed to suit our current conscious desires, but it must be done consciously and with intention and by concentrating on the Spirit within us rather than the desires of the ego. The real us is spirit; this conscious hidden intelligence that exists behind our eyes is timeless, formless and built from the magnificence of Source. It is not our name, our job, our home or our body; it is the I AM aspect of God.

We are pure spirit, cast into Human form as a manifestation of Divine Intelligence, existing for a little while on Earth as a Human to fulfill our part of the Divine Plan of God. There is only one intelligence, one mind, in all creation and every Human is a part of it. This Universal Mind knows no big or little, rich or poor, great or insignificant. It gives of itself and creates according to our desire and belief.

Think of this Mind, if you will, as a great plastic medium, containing all energy, all knowledge and all substance. Think of it as a medium responsive only to thought and responsive in degree and time according to how our thoughts are charged with desire, belief, expectancy, conviction, gratitude and desire.

Thoughts plus conviction equals manifestation.

There is manifested in our experience exactly that which we are convinced is possible. We need not remove all these negative prompters in a special procedure since positive will override negative. All that is necessary is for us to install in the Sub-conscious Mind a group of positive prompters through affirmations fueled by intention.

It is important that we pay close attention to our intuition and to not negate it whether it comes in a dream, repetitive thought, a flash of insight or something someone says to us that is the answer to something we have been questioning. We also need to pay attention to where our faith lies. What do we have faith in? People, money, government or God? Where our faith lies also lies our power to manifest.

Thought is the great creator, master and mother of the Universe, God in Humans, and the infinite in the immediate. There is no end to individual power through the right use of thought. Our sub-conscious negative prompters act as a closed door to the power of the great Universal Mind in which we live and move and have our being.

The complete removal of all negative prompters in mind, full contact with the Infinite, complete recognition of the Spiritual Laws and the spiritual nature of Humankind is the path provided for us to follow in our journey back to God. Once we admit there is a power greater than us and that we can connect with that power, we can use that power to create healthy, happy, abundant, loving lives. Every physical law of the Universe has a corresponding spiritual law.

Our bodies were created by our souls for their use. Our ego has convinced us to fear and that we are our bodies and has attempted to keep us from knowing ourselves as Spirit inhabiting a Human form. Our bodies are the embodiment of spirit, aspects of God, for the purpose of expressing God qualities in Human form.

There is a great medium of mind and intelligence that is in and surrounds every Human. This Intelligence is all and knows and does everything. This Intelligence, God, is an eternal Creator, creating that which the minds of Humans think. This invisible plane of Human existence offers the greatest challenge and the greatest hope of Humankind.

Change the idea of a thing and you change the thing.

Only you can be you. We are each created uniquely to come to Earth with unique attributes and missions. It does not serve us or our souls to attempt to be like anyone other than ourselves. We are to practice creativity instead of conformity and competition. Our security in life depends entirely on our recognition of our divine nature and contact with our soul.

We are told that even ten minutes a day spent in meditation affirming our divinity will change our lives for the better quicker than anything else we can do.

"In the beginning was the word," and it is with all creation, for the word is the thought. Speaking the word with conviction and maintaining that conviction with faith is the complete chain of manifestation from the thought to the thing. Faith is required; faith in God and faith in our own divinity. Make up your mind that the Intelligence that exists behind the Universe does not judge you or destroy Itself. Humankind has created evil and hell. We have Freewill and free choice to create evil, lack, disease and hatred. Or we can obtain good by creating good by the power of our faith and thoughts. God does not punish us. We punish ourselves by disobeying the Law of Karma, the law of Cause and Effect.

There are billions of Conscious Minds thinking into the Universal Mind, creating physical reality with each thought that is expressed with complete belief. The Universal Mind is reactive, creative and it can create for your neighbor or family what you think into it for them. And it tends to create for you what your neighbor and family thinks into it for you. The Universal Mind acts on the thought behind which there is the most belief and faith.

Believe you will fail and you will.
Believe you will succeed and you will.

Everything on this Earth is a result of thought. The Universal Mind attempts to manifest all thought to the person thinking it, and it also attempts to manifest it to the entire World. Every thought of every person who has ever lived has been indelibly recorded in Universal Mind which has been moved to action because of it. All thought is not consciously projected into the Creative Mind. Much of what gets expressed by Humans habitually and without deliberate thought becomes expressed. This is why monitoring what we are thinking at all times is so important. Universal Mind recognizes only conception and desire, or thought and emotion, and it recognizes them by creating them into actuality. We are all responsible for our thoughts and beliefs.

Besides Jesus, there have been many enlightened Humans who have lived on this planet. There have been societies of these enlightened Humans whose perception of truth has been so acute that physical manifestation from thought, thought transference and intuition has been common in their daily lives. Yet these Humans and societies have usually thought it dangerous to reveal this knowledge to Humanity as a whole. Jesus taught these same concepts in parables which have been misquoted and mistranslated in order to keep Humans believing we are powerless and sinners.

Through the Law of Attraction, all things come to those who believe in them. The quality of our lives is attracted to us by our beliefs and thoughts. Evil is the result of erroneous thought conception. Erroneous thought conception is the cause of Evil. The universe is owned and operated by a God of Love. Thoughts of a vengeful God and fear of God has been perpetrated by beings that wish to control others and is not based in truth.

It is important that we quit carrying around the burden of mistakes we believe we have made. It is important that we forgive ourselves and others and to begin to think positively.

We are not alone. We did not create ourselves. We cannot by ourselves do the slightest bit of creating. The power into which we project our thoughts is the only creative force there is. It builds and constructs all form and circumstances, but it does this according to how we think. This power creates what we believe and manifests for us what we can accept. We can create abundance in our experience only if we realize and know that there is abundance all about us and we accept it. In other words, we don't demand money, we don't force money with the idea that there is not enough to go around and we don't have enough of it. We accept money; there is a great abundance of it around us, and we know that. The force of our will against the Universal Mind must inevitably set up the same thing in our experience so that we see opposition instead of cooperation. Have confidence in the power greater than you are and have complete acceptance of good.

The power that creates is the power that knows; and it is possible, with perfect attunement, to achieve in each condition of your life a situation of guidance. When we completely accept the power greater than we are, when we know it will create our experience that which we believe, we will also find that it also will provide us with answers to our questions.

We must let go of our problems once the basic element of the problems are clearly defined in our Conscious Mind, and once our general objective is clearly defined in our Conscious Mind; we must let go. Forget the problem altogether. One morning while we are going about our daily tasks, we will find the solution. It will strike our consciousness with such impact as to remove all doubt it is truth.

There is guidance available. It is not achieved by effort or will. It is achieved by complete acceptance of the power greater than we are that knows the answer. The proper use of spiritual law is acceptance and faith. We are to seek balance between our Conscious Mind and our Sub-conscious Mind.

ACCEPT—BELIEVE—KNOW—RELAX—HAVE FAITH.

It has only been lately that scientists probing at the elemental substance of nature have yielded us the knowledge that mass and density are purely relative. The astounding discovery of science that there is no such thing as a solid mass has revised the thinking of the World. The only difference between us and what we think of as physical objects is our form of consciousness. There is only one substance from which everything physical is made, there is only one substance from which energy is made and this energy, or substance, is infinite in time and space; it has no beginning and no end and, thus, is everywhere at all times, and all of it is anywhere at any time. There is only one substance or energy or Intelligence in all things. Everything is basically one thing, has no beginning and no end, and has no past and no future, but only one eternal now.

The Sub-conscious Mind reacts entirely by suggestion and has no volition of its own. It does not by itself make choices, indulge in arguments, postulate theories, search for answers, wonder at possibilities. It only accepts and acts on suggestions from the Conscious Mind. It acts on those thoughts behind which there is the most conviction. Once it is given a suggestion, it immediately sets to work to make that suggestion truth, for it accepts that suggestion completely. Intuition is the aspect of mental power which enables a person to contact certain aspects of the Sub-conscious Mind through meditation. The contact comes when we get the Conscious Mind thoughts out of the way. All physical circumstance originates on the plane of thought.

We are to think in terms of complete unity. We are one with every person who lives, ever has lived, every form of life that exists, every inanimate object in our World, because all things are made from one thing. Thus, all things are one thing, and objects and circumstances exist as the result of conception and desire being projected into the infinite creative substance of which we are all a part, in which we are all one.

Thought is the only mover. According to the degree of our conscious intelligence, we will grasp the power that is ours. According to our conscious intelligence, we will project images into the Sub-conscious Mind thath we desire to experience. We must consciously exercise control over our thoughts.

The entire Universe is alive. There is nothing dead, nothing inanimate. When Jesus said, "God is not a God of the dead but a God of the living," He was revealing the basic truth of all creation For all is living and all is intelligence and all is conscious; and the great motivating force of all life is its attempt to expand its consciousness. In other words, it seeks to know itself. Evolution is life expanding to a conscious oneness with God. It is useful to think, "I Am that, I AM."

It can be said that the purpose of life is the attainment of knowledge, the expansion of consciousness, a constant reaching upward and outward and inward toward a Oneness with God. As the Spirit expands its consciousness, it seeks a new form through which to express itself. The body which you now occupy is but an instrument of your consciousness and expression of your knowledge of yourself. By the very nature of your being, your consciousness must grow and, as it does, your Spirit will gradually lay down your current body and return again into the Universal Consciousness where it starts anew in its quest for a new expression. The level we go to when we leave these bodies matches the level of consciousness we have attained in this life.

Other Books by bj King

Pentimento: Diary of a Walk-In

Self-Mastery Of Mind And Emotion

Who Are You And What On Earth Are You

Life After Life

Old Loves Are Seldom Finished ... When New Loves Begin

I Am Presence and Violet Flame

The Universal Laws and Jesus' Meaning of The Beatitudes

Manual for Spiritual Maturity

The Master Jesus Speaks

Life is A Spiritual Game

Principles of Truth

www.ingramcontent.com/pod-product-compliance
Lightning Source LLC
Chambersburg PA
CBHW020358170426
43200CB00005B/212